# UNASSAILABLE

## DEFEND YOURSELF FROM DEPLATFORM ATTACKS, CANCEL CULTURE & OTHER ONLINE DISASTERS

### MARK E. JEFTOVIC

# CONTENTS

## ACKNOWLEDGMENTS_

A lot of people helped me with this book and I'd like to take this opportunity to mention them in no particular order:

Sieg Pedde, Osama Arafat , Jim Carroll and Jesse Hirsh all read initial drafts and helped me flesh it out. Leslie James proof read it, more than once.

Always appreciative of Tamas Acs and Ranko Rodic who basically run the business while I write books, as well as the entire crew at easyDNS who do their jobs admirably.

And lastly, especially, my wife Angela who helped me stay focused on the subject material.

To Prometheus, the first whistleblower.

   And for today's dissidents, indie media, whistleblowers, contrarians and anybody else who speaks truth to power at great risk.

"Everyone has the right to freedom of opinion and expression; this right includes freedom to hold opinions without interference and to seek, receive and impart information and ideas through any media and regardless of frontiers."

FOREWORD_
BY CHARLES HUGH SMITH
(OFTWOMINDS.COM)

Societies around the world are experiencing unprecedented cultural purges of ideas and narratives that challenge the status quo. In some nations, this purge is managed by the central government, China being a leading example. In the developed Western nations, this purge is being conducted by private for-profit technology platforms that function as quasi-monopolies in Internet search, video and advertising (Google) and social media (Facebook and Twitter). Other technology platforms that provide communications and monetization of content services can also squelch free thought and expression by deleting accounts or *shadow-banning* content: they maintain the appearance of free access to the platform but severely limit its distribution. Just because you see your post doesn't mean anyone else can see it or forward it to others.

This empowering of corporations to conduct society-wide censorship without any legal protections is an extraordinarily dangerous precedent. Any user can be banned for what I call "Anti-Soviet Thought," a reference to the Soviet Union's Orwellian-Kafkaesque system of conducting show trials and imprisoning citizens for "thought crimes." A content creator banned by a tech platform has no rights or recourse: the platform is not obligated to identify the "crime" that supposedly violated their User Agreement or present evidence in support of this accusation. The banned user has no means to contest the "conviction" or the "sentence" (which as Mark so aptly describes, is a form of social and financial invisibility.)

In effect, these tech platforms wield extra-legal powers that are impervious to conventional government protections of civil liberties. (Those who attempt to sue these corporations face legal teams larger than those serving government agencies.) Users agree to open-ended Terms of Service that the corporations can interpret however they please, without any transparent process of appeal or redress.

Historically, dissident voices tended to find safe harbor in academia and the media: it's difficult to fire tenured professors over their public opinions, and the pre-internet (and often family owned) media jealously guarded the independence of its journalists.

Today, the cultural purge is sweeping through these sectors with a vengeance. It's increasingly difficult to obtain tenure, and the traditional media has been bought up by corporations that have gutted employment as advertising revenues declined. (Recall that six corporations own the vast majority of the mainstream media, and they are enthusiastic fellow travelers of the cultural purge.)

In response, dissenting voices turned to the internet's alternative media space of blogs, forums, podcasts and websites. In the pre-platform-monopoly days of the early 2000s, this space seemed to be a bulwark against censorship. The rise of these platforms has effectively brought the alternative media under their control: a content creator can still host a website but distribution and monetization (i.e. earning income from the content) are largely controlled by the platforms.

This suppression of dissenting views is enormously dangerous to democracy and the economy, as maintaining a diverse ecosystem of competing ideas and enterprises is the lifeblood of both democracy and free enterprise. We're not just fighting to maintain our intellectual and financial independence, we're also fighting for civil society and a vibrant economy that isn't stifled by monopolies and cartels.

I am an unwilling expert on the mechanics of shadow-banning, since my content has been actively shadow-banned or limited by Facebook and Twitter. (Google's fingerprints are harder to see.) The idea behind shadow-banning is especially pernicious, as the intent is to promote the illusion of openness while crippling the content creator financially by limiting access to the platform's hundreds of millions of users.

I consider my content to be self-evidently reasonable. Indeed, I often half-jokingly point out that the primary data source on my site is the Federal Reserve of St. Louis database (FRED). My point is that reasonableness and data are no defense against purges, censorship and shadow-banning. We all need a well-thought out strategy to maintain our independence and our income, and this is what Mark lays out in these pages.

Mark explains why these defenses are necessary, and then lays out how to implement them. The entire strategy may feel overwhelming; if so, view it as a roadmap: start with the most critical defenses of your independence, and then make progress as time, money and effort allow.

The alternative media space is changing fast as the platforms seek to consolidate their power and co-opt, discredit or disempower their increasingly numerous critics. The business model of earning a livelihood from advertisements that seemed relatively secure has disintegrated before our eyes. We must expect further disruptions of distribution and monetization, and our only real defense is to control our own *capital*: the intellectual capital of our content, the social capital of our audience and network, and the economic capital of our revenue sources and income streams.

Our first job is to survive: maintain our content creation, our distribution of that content and whatever income we generate from our audience. Democracy and free enterprise need us to survive, and Mark's book gives us a roadmap to not just survive but prosper.

Charles Hugh Smith
　　https://oftwominds.com
　　9/25/19

# INTRODUCTION_

---

The Rule of Opinion differs from all other kinds of rule in that it requires the continuous coexistence of opposing opinions, hence it avoids the most deadly sort of dogmatism that crushes by violence other faiths in the certainty of its own righteousness. In a democracy men still cherish their dogmas, but not to the extent of destroying other men for their contrary dogmatism.

- ROBERT M. MACIVER, THE WEB OF GOVERNMENT,<br>1947.

---

Unfortunately, this book is for a lot of people. One I wish I didn't feel compelled to write. Too often we hear about content creators being censored on the internet. The reason why is because people who disagree with them embark on deplatforming campaigns and are successful.

Rather than either personally rejecting an idea or content one finds unpalatable, or rebutting such ideas with one's own voice, people seem to be OK with the idea that they enjoy some exalted moral status that means *they* should get to decide if anybody *else* should be able to create or access targeted content.

This book is for anybody who earns their living online. While primarily it is for content creators, many of the principles in this book can be used by any business that relies heavily on their internet presence, and as such must take measures to remain online at all times.

Even if you are a content creator who assumes nothing you say is controversial enough to attract a deplatforming campaign, bear in mind that what seems reasonable today may be considered beyond the pale tomorrow. Further, by assuming the type of defensive posture outlined in this book, you will also be protected against other types of outages, such as key vendors disappearing via business shutdown or technological misadventure.

In other words, the impetus and focus of this book is to mitigate deplatforming attacks, but it is also a general informal disaster recovery blueprint.

If you're not super technical, that's fine. This book is written for the generalist. The important part is to make the mind shift to a decentralized, defensive posture under your own nominal control and ownership.

---

This book was originally intended to be a 15 or 20 page ebook I was going to use as a subscriber magnet to garner opt-ins to my company's #AxisOfEasy weekly newsletter[1].

Over the summer of 2019 I became more concerned every time I listened to another podcast or heard a tale of somebody being deplatformed, so I kept adding additional sections. Then I found myself writing about the history, the philosophy and the ethos behind culture wars in general. While easily a topic for another book entirely, it wound up in here, and I'm loathe to move it.

There's enough of that to split this book into two parts. In the first part I wax philosophical about culture wars and the importance of narrative control, then in the second part we dive right into what you do to protect yourself from the legions of hysterical pearl clutchers. If you have no interest in the navel gazing, then feel free to skip straight to the second part.

There are a few places where we may get technical. If so then simply hand this book over or forward it to your resident techie or consultant, or whomever you presently rely upon to "do all the web stuff". They'll know what to do.

Only ideas can overcome ideas.

- LUDWIG VON MISES

There can be only one permanent revolution — a moral one; the regeneration of the inner man. How is this revolution to take place? Nobody knows how it will take place in humanity, but every man feels it clearly in himself. *And yet in our world everybody thinks of changing humanity, and nobody thinks of changing himself.*

- LEO TOLSTOY

# FREEDOM IS A TWO-EDGED SWORD_

---

"Freedom is a two-edged sword of which one edge is liberty and the other, responsibility. Both edges are exceedingly sharp and the weapon is not suited to casual, cowardly or treacherous hands."

- JACK PARSONS

---

In 1946, a rather eccentric rocket scientist named Jack Parsons penned an essay about the nature of freedom. He noted that for the majority of human history, the norm was slavery. It was considered beyond challenge that some, indeed most, of the members of society were quite literally born to serve a much smaller minority of elites. Their souls were owned by God, and thus subject to the clergy, while their bodies were the State's, to do with as it pleased;

---

For numberless centuries society accepted the proposition that certain men were created to be slaves. Their natural function was to serve priests, kings and nobles, men of substance and property who were appointed slave-masters by almighty God. This system was reinforced by the established doctrine that all men and women were owned 'in mind' by the church and 'in body' by the state. This convenient situation was supported by the authority of social morality, religion and even philosophy.

Against this doctrine, some two hundred years ago, rose the most astonishing heresy the world has yet seen; the principle of liberalism. In essence this principle stated that all men are created equal and endowed with inalienable rights which belong to every man as his birthright.[1]

---

Parsons laments that since this heretical notion of classical liberalism took the world by storm, various authorities have sought to co-opt the idea of liberty to suit their own agendas:

---

[Freedom] has since made some headway in spite of the opposition of the majority of organized society. As a slogan, however, it has become so popular that it is rendered unwilling lip-service by all the major states and yet it is still so distasteful to persons in authority that it is nowhere embodied as a fundamental law and is continually violated in letter and in spirit by every trick of bigotry and reaction. Further, absolutist and totalitarian groups of the most vicious nature use liberalism as a cloak under which they move to re-establish tyrannies and to extinguish the liberty of all who oppose them.

Thus religious groups seek to abrogate freedom of art, speech and the press; reactionaries move to suppress labor, communists to establish dictatorships -- and all in the name of 'freedom'. Because of the peculiar definitions of freedom used by some of these camouflaged tyrants, it seems necessary to redefine Freedom in the terms understood by Voltaire, Paine, Washington, Jefferson and Emerson. [2]

---

Given that freedom is a two-edged sword, I invoke Parsons here to serve the dual ramifications of writing a book like this. It's a given that *Unassailable* is written with the intent to give content creators a toolkit to defend their ideas and their liveli-hood from those who would seek not only to suppress their ideas but to even derail their careers.

But there may also be those who may level the admonition that writing a book like this empowers the wrong sorts of people to promulgate wrong-headed ideas, who would then be able to resist efforts of right-thinking people to compel them to shut the hell up.

What these critics fail to understand is that it is not their prerogative to decide what is right-headed or wrong-headed *for anybody other than themselves*. It's really this simple:

---

No man, no group and no nation has the right to any man's individual freedom. No matter how pure the motive, how great the emergency, how high the principle, such action is nothing but tyranny. It is never justified.

The question is: are we able to face the consequences of democracy?[3]

---

Everybody has the freedom, and dare I say *the responsibility,* to assess whether ideas are right or wrong for themselves.

In practical terms, truly bad ideas with no redeeming qualities, such as real actual racism or its myriad variations of intolerance are uniformly abhorred by the vast majority of classical liberal society . These strains of thought are largely dying out under their own impetus, in some places quickly, others more slowly. Overall, society is becoming less intolerant and more inclusive with each successive generation.

Anybody who feels that they are qualified to decide what other people should be permitted to read or write, or hear or think should instead expend their effort on improving *themselves,* before they tackle outside world. The only thing you can really change about the external world is what you bring into it. Nobody among us is perfect, so there is always something we can work on internally. That's the core truth behind the famous adage *"be the change you want to see in the world".*

The rockstar psychologist Jordan B Peterson put it quite succinctly in this short excerpt from a panel he participated in on Australia's Q&A[4] show (we look at JBP shortly in Chapter 4: Does Deplatforming Even Work?)

---

"My experience has been that people can do a tremendous amount of good for themselves and for the people who are immediately around them by looking to their own inadequacies and their own flaws and the things that they're not doing in their lives and starting to build themselves up as more powerful individuals.

If they're capable of doing that then they're capable

of expanding their career. If they're capable of expanding their career and their competence then they're capable of taking their place in the community as effective leaders.

Then they're capable of making a wise decision instead of an unwise decision when it comes to making collective political decisions.

I'm not suggesting, and I've never suggested that there's no domain for social action. I'm suggesting that people who don't have their own houses in order should be careful before they go about re-organizing the world"

---

You have the freedom to pay no attention to ideas that bother you.

You have the freedom to intellectually or creatively rebut ideas you disagree with.

You have the freedom to evangelize for a competing or alternative idea to those you disagree with.

*You have no right to infringe on anybody else's right to peacefully express their own ideas or thoughts. Even if you think they are bad ones.*

Jack Parsons had a complex personality and was admittedly a bit of a mixed-bag. He was a self-proclaimed Thelemic magician and a disciple of Aleister Crowley, the so-called "Wickedest Man in the World" of his era.

He was also a prolific scientific engineer for the military industrial complex, and at one time was Scientology founder L. Ron Hubbard's landlord. Hubbard ran off with Parson's girlfriend while simultaneously grifting him for most of his savings.[5]

His unorthodox past helps make the wider point: you are free to do what you want, provided you're willing to accept the consequences of whatever you do. Parsons died young, having been run out of his profession by rabid McCarthyism, the deplatform attacks of his day. Forced to practice his vocation in a homegrown laboratory, he was killed by an explosion at his Pasadena residence in 1957. He was 37.

Parsons is a good example of another dynamic we see play out all too often in the contemporary culture wars, the idea that the eccentricities and misadventures of a given personality make or break what that person has said or is trying to say. This is a type of logical fallacy known as "poisoning the well", and it gets used *a lot* when Social Justice Warriors go after a given target with the goal of deplatforming them.

---

If this book gets any noticeable coverage it will no doubt come under criticism. In it, we will be providing tools and methodologies to those who would seek to defend themselves from other people's moral judgements. For that, it's possible we will be accused of "enabling hate", "normalizing" something social justice warriors dislike intensely, or some other form of wrongthink.

Somebody may claim that Irredeemable Miscreants may read this book and employ the knowledge herein to defend their content from deplatforming initiatives.

But the problem with cancel culture is that Irredeemable Miscreants also buy MacBook Pro laptops, they may drive to Irredeemable Miscreant rallies in Teslas and eat vegan soy patties. The only way to truly guarantee the sterility of all interactions would be through the enactment of a top-down command-and-control society in which nobody can do anything until everybody involved can prove their moral purity. It quickly becomes dystopian, which is why even a hypothetical impulse toward this "ideal" should be resisted on all fronts.

There are far scarier things in the culture wars of today than Irredeemable Miscreants. Whoever those may be, they are almost certainly a minuscule rabble of dysfunctional fringe types who would be completely irrelevant if it weren't for the incessant din of hysterics shrieking about how awful they are.

There is only magic bullet that is guaranteed to kill a truly irredeemable idea, and that is *disinterest*. We'll explore this further in Chapter 4, "Does Deplatforming Even Work?"


## USE YOUR POWERS FOR GOOD

What I do hope is that once armed with the information you will learn in this book, you will use it to fight injustice, ideological overreach and malignant groupthink.

The real threats today have names like "the greater good", "the science is settled", "that's a conspiracy theory" and any other variation on a theme that some people feel it's within their purview to decide what ideas are acceptable for everybody else, and more perniciously, that any disagreement is illegitimate and not permissible.


Those people are wrong. And for those of you whom they will come at next, it's for you that I've written this book.

# INVISIBLE MEN ARE NOT WELCOME IN THE PANOPTICON_



In the 1963 short story by Robert Silverberg *To See The Invisible Man*, Mitch Chaplin is sentenced to one year of "invisibility" for his crime of "coldness" toward his fellow man. In the original print version we learn it is Mitch's fourth such offence. The protagonist initially thought the sentence somewhat comical and that it would amount to a year long vacation. The story was made into a television episode in the first season of the 1980s' Twilight Zone reboot, wherein Chaplin exclaims in glee "I can do a year on a pogo stick!".

The TV version for the most part tracks the short story quite closely. The sentence quickly takes its psychological toll on our antihero as he realizes that he cannot interact with society in even the most routine ways. Deprived of all interactions and services he finds himself living a hellish wraith-like existence. Chaplin meets another invisible, male in the short story, female in the TV version, and in each case begs them to acknowledge him as a fellow traveller, which neither of them does.

After his sentence has been served, and Chaplin rejoins society, he re-encounters the same invisibles who previously shunned him. In both narratives, his compassion gets the better of him and he communicates with his compadres, *"I can see you!"*, albeit now setting himself up for an even longer, five year term of invisibility.

Chaplin faced a state imposed penalty of societal shunning. We can infer from our vantage point in the early 21st century that his crime of "coldness toward his fellow man" was an indictment of individualism and personal liberty. His "coldness" was his rejection of groupthink and collectivism.

While we here in the West we are not yet systemically shunned this way for this reason, China is perfecting a technocratic system called Sesame Credit which does bring this type of automated diminishment to those who run afoul of the rules[1].

Citizens in China who face sanctions under this system are penalized for being late paying bills, for jaywalking, for purchasing alcohol too frequently, or for any number of suboptimal behaviours as deemed so by state authorities. Consequences include being unable to purchase train or air traffic tickets, inability to get one's child into preferred schools, denial of credit facilities. The system is deployed already and was originally targeted to become compulsory for all citizens of China sometime in 2020[2].

Again, we here in the West are not subject to such stringent control of our behaviours *yet*. But given the willingness of Western tech companies, such as Google and IBM to supply the infrastructure to facilitate the Chinese surveillance state[3], I am apprehensive that what occurs there will eventually manifest here, albeit in a characteristically westernized dialect.

For now we are under intense social pressure to conform to pre-approved narratives of both thought and discourse.

The boundaries of this Overton Window are governed by a perhaps vocal minority relative to the wider population. However, they do control the major choke points of the opinion shaping apparatus of mass media and social networks. It is not officially State sanctioned, but it presents as a more-or-less uniform ideology.

The phenomenon I'm describing has been described by other commentators from across the ideological spectrum. I believe it's what Jaron Lanier meant when he described "Digital Maoism" in his 2006 essay for The Edge magazine:

---

[T]he problem is in the way [the online collective] has come to be regarded and used; how it's been elevated to such importance so quickly. And that is part of the larger pattern of the appeal of a new online collectivism that is nothing less than a resurgence of the idea that the collective is all-wise, that it is desirable to have influence concentrated in a bottleneck that can channel the collective with the most verity and force. This is different from representative democracy, or meritocracy. This idea has had dreadful consequences when thrust upon us from the extreme Right or the extreme Left in various historical periods.

- HTTPS://WWW.EDGE.ORG/CONVERSATION/

George Gilder called it "Google Marxism" in his "Life After Google"(2019) which Michael Rectenwald then used as a departure point and expanded it into "The Google Archipelago" in his book by the same name.

Rectenwald, in his book, cites the post-modernist Michel Foucault and his concept of "The Panopticon": an all seeing prison construct where everyone is observed, however the observers are not. Foucault posited a society where instead of prisons becoming panopticons, panopticons would envelope society itself:

"Panopticism" describes a transmutation in the expression and exercise of power that took place from the pre-modern to the modern period. This change included a shift away from primarily corporal forms of punishment—torture, quartering, branding and other brutal rituals for inflicting bodily pain—but also power's decentralization, its metastasis and permeation of the entire society—its effects no longer confined to the imprisoned, insane, or otherwise detained. The new "disciplinary" regime included the reformed prisons and other places of confinement but also escaped the confines of institutions to become applied universally to the entire population. *The whole society became a disciplinary society.*

- MICHAEL RECTENWALD. GOOGLE ARCHIPELAGO: THE

DIGITAL GULAG AND THE SIMULATION OF FREEDOM
(EMPHASIS ADDED)

The sharp end of the the stick of The Panopticon is cancel culture, facilitated by roving bands of hair-triggered social justice warriors, scouring the internet for any hint of offensive opinions, behaviours or content. Whether in the present or in your distant past, anything that could be deemed offensive, omniphobic[4] or problematic will be uncovered, recontextualized as required, in some cases fabricated entirely, and then amplified.

This circumscribes and sequesters for exclusion all heterodox opinion, and the penalties called for are increasingly that the offending party be deplatformed and cancelled. This era's version of being pronounced invisible.

Contrast with our earlier Twilight Zone episode, there is no trial, no due process and no formal procedure of rendering a citizen invisible. Not to mention there is not the tradition of taking the reformed invisible out for a sociable drink upon completion of their sentence. This latter point is an important one: not only are you cancelled without due process, once you have been cancelled there is no road back.

There is just a flash mob of hysterical rage, directed not only at the target, but also at their vendors, clients, partners and the media demanding that the condemned have their technical support, platform access and financial lifeblood summarily withdrawn by anybody remotely connected to them, lest *they too* be branded with the mark of Cain: an arbitrary and summary designation that they are "intolerant", "offensive" or that they "support hate".

If you're producing content today that runs contrary to what the Libertarian historian Tom Woods[5] calls *"the 3 by 5 index card of allowable opinion"*, you run the real risk that your ideological opponents will not be content with rebutting what you say with their own voice within the marketplace of ideas.

Rather, the tactic of deplatforming one's opponents is seen as a legitimate response to an unapproved viewpoint, because in the prevailing orthodoxy, anything that doesn't conform to The Panopticon's sensibilities is by definition illegitimate. Anyone who advances an orthogonal opinion forfeits their right to publish any opinion at all.

Many businesses and personalities have seen their audiences decimated, their followings revoked and their access to payment systems and financial resources strangled because they found themselves to be deplatformed by their ideological opponents.

## CANCEL CULTURE THROUGH THE AGES_

---

Whoever would overthrow the liberty of a nation must begin by subduing the freeness of speech

- BENJAMIN FRANKLIN

---

Among the most ardent deplatformers there seems a conspicuous absence of historical awareness. But cancel culture is nothing new. In more ancient times, unapproved opinions or inconvenient facts were subject to brutal repression, both for those who produced them and those who consumed them.

In 1764, Voltaire wrote *"It is better to have to do with a single tyrant than will a whole pack of little tyrants"* in his *Dictionaire Philosophique,* which the French Parliament took to mean themselves and ordered his book burned by the hangman.[1] In our era "a whole pack of little tyrants" has a more literal meaning.

The most burned book throughout all history is The Talmud. Throughout long swaths of history it was the Jews who were the invisibles, widely denied the right to have even an opinion on matters....

---

'The thirteenth century controversy amongst the Jews regarding rabbi-philosopher Maimonides and his *Sefer HaMadda (Book of Knowledge)* and *Moreh Nevukhim (Code for the Perplexed)* spilled over into the Catholic Church's search for heretical beliefs...Traditional rabbinic scholars disproved of Maimonides' books and "decreed that any person found reading them was to be banned and his property confiscated. In their indignation they turned to the church authorities, ..., condemned the Maimonidean philosophic books to the flames" (Saracheck 86)'[2]

---

During the myriad cases of book burnings throughout antiquity, it was not uncommon for the author or the author's proponents to be extinguished alongside the damning material.

---

'In 1624, Marco Antonio de Dominis was condemned by the Inquisition for his criticisms and attacks on some practices of the Church and it was ordered "to deprive him all his honour, benefit or dignity; to confiscate his goods; and give him over to the secular powers, as *de facto*. They then gave him over, that he and his picture, together with a little sack of bookes he had printed, should be burned" (Gillette 1932 119-120). On December 21, 1624, de Dominis, his picture and books were burned at Campo di Fiori in Rome'.[3]

---

Heretical authors were not always burned along with their books, although when they were, it was often with their books hung about their necks with rope. Sometimes they were merely imprisoned, exiled, or hanged, drawn and quartered, or had their hands or ears cut off.[4]

It is a common analogy today to compare deplatformings to book burnings of yore. I've made that comparison myself. But as I wrote this (which was originally intended to be a free ebook no more than 15 or 20 pages) I came to realize that analogy is not entirely accurate. The book burnings are akin to the deletion of an account, or a website takedown. But that doesn't capture the entire ethos.

Culture wars are all about narrative control. Whoever can shape or influence the current trajectory has the ability to steer the entire zeitgeist. Edward Bernays, the nephew of Sigmund Freud and the father of modern propaganda, understood the necessity of molding the prevailing narrative:

> The conscious and intelligent manipulation of the organized habits and opinions of the masses is an important element in democratic society. Those who manipulate this unseen mechanism of society constitute an invisible government which is the true ruling power of our country. We are governed, our minds are molded, our tastes formed, our ideas suggested, largely by men we have never heard of. This is a logical result of the way in which our democratic society is organized. Vast

numbers of human beings must cooperate in this manner if they are to live together as a smoothly functioning society. Our invisible governors are, in many cases, unaware of the identity of their fellow members in the inner cabinet. They govern us by their qualities of natural leadership, their ability to supply needed ideas and by their key position in the social structure. Whatever attitude one chooses to take toward this condition, it remains a fact that in almost every act of our daily lives, whether in the sphere of politics or business, in our social conduct or our ethical thinking, we are dominated by the relatively small number of persons—a trifling fraction of our hundred and twenty million—who understand the mental processes and social patterns of the masses. It is they who pull the wires which control the public mind, who harness old social forces and contrive new ways to bind and guide the world.

- EDWARD BERNAYS, PROPAGANDA, 1928

---

Bernays was clearly an elitist, and he unapologetically considered the public to be a rabble. The opening words of his book, Propaganda, which we quoted somewhat at length above, was titled "Organizing Chaos". Thus, propaganda comprises techniques and strategies to push elite approved narratives into the public mind and to have them accepted. Bernays deemed this a necessity of a smooth operating society.

The other side of controlling the narrative necessitates the suppression of any contending streams of thought. That's where deplatforming comes in.

The ramifications of successfully asserting one trajectory over any other challengers may never be fully grasped by the public at large.

Over the history of Christianity, narratives were decided in Ecumenical Councils, and even then, cancel culture had its analogs.

For example, at the Ecumenical Council of 869 it was decided what the nature of man was in spiritual terms. "The Council of 869 robbed mankind of its spiritual consciousness[5]", when it was decided that man, who up until that point was held within Christianity to be a threefold creature, consisting of mind, body and *spirit*, was henceforth decreed to be a duality.

Body and mind, that's it. Or else…

---

At the time when the 'Ecumenical Council' at Constantinople decreed that man's nature was twofold _ body and soul —, Scot Eriugena proclaimed that the human being is composed of body, soul and Spirit, and that the Spirit is eternal. It does not completely embody itself in one particular incarnation of the soul, said Scot Eriugena, but goes through many successive incarnations on its path towards perfection. It does so in accordance with the divine laws that govern the development of man. After the decree of 869, Scot Eriugena was accused of heresy and, according to popular tradition, having become Abbot of Malmesbury he was finally condemned by his own students who stabbed him to death with their pens.

- PAUL EMBERSO, FROM GONDHISHAPUR TO SILICON VALLEY, VOL 1. 2009

---

The common theme throughout events of this nature are that the crimes are heretical as opposed to tangible. These persecutions occurred because of what their victims said, not what they did. They were all thought crimes.

A precedent setting historical event in that narrative control became the objective in itself was The French Revolution. In particular, the point *after* which it successfully overthrew the monarchy, it began to cannibilize itself as the revolutionaries turned on themselves,

---

The trial of the Girondists followed immediately upon that of the Queen. The general charge was conspiracy against the unity and indivisibility of the republic. *These men had dared to recommend a different public policy from that of the blind fanatics who were now in power —that was their real crime.* How far removed were those dreams of liberty, those broken yokes and sundered chains, that filled the minds of the first Revolutionists! The rights of man, where now were they? *The very essence of the parliamentary system is that men may not be called to account for honest opinions they may have expressed in debate.* Yet now, every old grievance of the Mountain against the Gironde was aired anew. *There was no attempt at a legal conviction for conspiracy. The only proofs adduced were utterances in the National Assembly, in the press, or in private letters that had been seized.*

- ERNEST F. HENDERSON, SYMBOL AND SATIRE IN THE FRENCH REVOLUTION, 1912 *(EMPHASIS ADDED)*

---

The Girondists were found guilty of crimes against the

Revolution and followed the royals to the guillotine, kicking off the chapter in history we now refer to as The Terror.

---

Fortunately, today we don't pay for our heterodoxy with our lives, at least not yet. We have had state sanctioned murder of whistleblowers or dissident journalists, such as the Saudi Arabian government's brutal murder of Jamal Khashoggi[6]. And we have the UK and US treatment of Julian Assange who looks like he will possibly die while in custody[7].

But for the moment, here in the West, espousing a non-conforming opinion is not a capital offence. However deplatforming still aims to deny the offender of any basic claims to legitimacy within the societal structure itself. It's not enough to burn the books, or suspend the Twitter account. You have to make the dissident voice persona non grata entirely. If they had a book deal in the works, get it spiked. A talk show? Target the advertisers until the network drops the show. A website? Lean on the host until they take it *down.*

---

As a rule, these attacks, regardless of whether the ostensible impetus is religious, or scientific or even philosophical are, at their core, are *political* acts. Deplatforming today is not necessarily akin to the actual book burnings of yesteryear, but more accurately the *denial of service,* "a DoS attack"[8] to their authors, such as exile, excommunication, or execution.

---

In contemporary times, because of our obsession with the present and our eagerness to ignore or revise history to suit the current ideological fashion, we tend to forget that this is more the rule than the exception. In a 1950 preface to his "Freedom is a Two-Edged Sword", our previously cited Jack Parsons observed that:

---

"Since I first wrote this essay in 1946, some of the more ominous predictions have been fulfilled. Public employees have been subjected to the indignity of "loyalty" oaths and the ignominy of loyalty purges.

Members of the United States Senate, moving under the cloak of immunity and the excuse of emergency, have made a joke of justice and a mockery of privacy. Constitutional immunity and legal procedure have been consistently violated and that which once would have been an outrage in America is today refused even a review by the Supreme Court."

---

Sound familiar? Alas, even McCarthyism is nostalgia now. Our current day analogs have no compunction against using tried-and-true scorched earth tactics to bring about utter ruination of their targets with an objective to completely cancel their ability to interact with today's digital civilization, even in the most mundane way.

These days the heterodox aren't burned at the stake *literally*, however the destruction of one's livelihood for promulgating wrongthink is very much on the table.

# DOES DEPLATFORMING EVEN WORK?_



So far we've talked about the trade-off between liberty and one's responsibility to accept the consequences of being endowed with it. We've examined the The Panopticon, which is a term for the ubiquitous scrunity and enforcement of unwritten rules that set the boundaries of permissible dialogue, a.k.a "The Overton Window". We've looked back through history and surmised that perhaps what we are experiencing today is simply an extension of an endless contest for narrative control between various factions of vested interests.

But before we get into the strategic and tactical considerations of how to parry deplatform attacks, we need to ask one final, crucial question. Does deplatforming even work? What about their close cousin, the boycott?

In my experience, I've found that attempting to suppress the ideas, content and actions of others has the exact opposite effect of the stated aims of the initiative.

When such gatekeepers step in, the effort of telling everybody else what is right or wrong frequently backfires, and what happens instead is The Streisand Effect.

## THE STREISAND EFFECT

The term was coined by Techdirt editor Mike Masnick,[1] who took inspiration from a 2005 incident involving entertainer Barbra Streisand. A photographer took photos of her Malibu home without her permission, and she sued him for violation of privacy. The ensuing publicity garnered far more exposure of the photos of said beach house, thus reducing her privacy. Masnick called it "The Streisand Effect".

> How long is it going to take before lawyers realize that the simple act of trying to repress something they don't like online is likely to make it so that something that most people would *never, ever* see (like a photo of a urinal in some random beach resort) is now seen by many more people? Let's call it the **Streisand Effect.**[2]

Masnick hit on a universal truth of sorts. In 1912, the Russian mathematician and esotericist P. D. Ouspensky wrote in Tertium Organum:

> "[T]ry to destroy an idea by effort. The more you fight against it, the more you argue, refute, ridicule it, the more the idea will grow, spread and gain strength. On the other hand, silence, oblivion, non-doing, 'non-resistance' will annihilate, or at any rate weaken the idea."

---

This timeless insight seems like it should be nearly self-evident. Yet it remains inexplicably and stubbornly ungrasped by many of the sorts who take it upon themselves to deplatform those whose opinions or ideals they dislike.

## THERE'S NO SUCH THING AS BAD PRESS

The late great Canadian record producer Jack Richardson, when he was a college professor commenting on potential effects of bad publicity once told me, "Mark, the only thing that matters is that they get the band's name right. That's it."

I was asking him for advice because I was worried that a publicity stunt the heavy-metal band I was in at the time was about to spin out of control[3]. He told me it would have been the best possible outcome if it did. It didn't, and the band fizzled into obscurity, forcing me to stick with life plan B (which was working with computers).

Boycotts can and do have negative effects on incumbent, well known brands. But for the comparatively unknown or niche brands and those personalities who are not household names, boycotts may actually have a positive counter-effect in that they garner more widespread brand awareness.

A 2009 paper co-authored by two professors from Stanford Business School and one from Wharton found that "negative publicity should have differential effects on established versus unknown products."[4]

It's a brutally pragmatic calculation to make, but from my observations, when an ideologically based backlash or boycott ensues, either nothing changes or the target actually benefits from the counter-reaction. I've often suspected that the larger dynamic here is the Streisand Effect or just brand repetition.

---

"Through increasing awareness, negative publicity may increase sales when product awareness or accessibility is low. If few people know about a book released by a new author, any publicity, regardless of valence, should increase awareness. Although it focuses more on accessibility than awareness, this suggestion is analogous to work by Nedungadi (1990) showing that cues, which activate related brands, only have effects in situations where consideration is unlikely without a reminder. In addition, **negative publicity may be even more likely to boost sales if awareness and publicity valence become dissociated in memory.** Similar to the sleeper effect (Hannah and Sternthal 1984), where source information tends to become dissociated from the message over time, people may have a feeling of awareness, or remember they heard something about the product, but the valence may be forgotten (also see Skurnik et al. 2005). Work on advertising, for example, theorizes that **even negative ads might boost purchase likelihood after delay because it increases brand awareness** (Moore and Hutchinson 1983, 1985).

- POSITIVE EFFECTS OF NEGATIVE PUBLICITY: WHEN NEGATIVE REVIEWS INCREASE SALES, 2009 BY JONAH BERGER, ALAN T. SORENSEN & SCOTT J. RASMUSSEN. (EMPHASIS ADDED)

What this means is if you're on the receiving end of some boycott or cancel culture initiative now, and thousands or millions of people hear your name *for the first time* but have no investment with you one way or the other, it may not necessarily be a bad thing for you. Months later when they need whatever it is you sell, and they enumerate the existing options in their minds, you may make the list and they won't even remember why.

Despite this, boycotts and deplatformings continue, yet the counter-effects and backfires from them continue to mutate and surprise.

## THE TIMES FACEBOOK & TWITTER CANCELLED FREE THOUGHT

I knew about the Free Thought Project[5] and Police the Police for some time, having seen their content shared across numerous Facebook groups I participate in and across Twitter.

What I didn't realize was that they had been among the earliest targets of coordinated deplatformings. One day I simply stopped seeing their content. In retrospect, Twitter especially reminds me of the venerable children's tale Watership Down. The rabbits, in search of a new home, come to a seemingly idyllic warren inhabited by other seemingly friendly rabbits. They are welcomed to stay, there is food aplenty and lush meadows. The only problem is, every once in a while one of the rabbits goes missing, and nobody is allowed to ask why. That's social media today...

And since they could not bear the truth, these singers,

who might in some other place have been wise, were squeezed under the terrible weight of the warren's secret until they gulped out fine folly—about dignity and acquiescence, and anything else that could make believe that the rabbit loved the shining wire. But one strict rule they had; oh yes, the strictest. No one must ever ask where another rabbit was and anyone who asked 'Where?'—except in a song or a poem—must be silenced. To say 'Where?' was bad enough, but to speak openly of the wires—that was intolerable. For that they would scratch and kill."

> - ADAMS, RICHARD. WATERSHIP DOWN: A NOVEL (PUFFIN BOOKS BOOK 1) (P. 104). SCRIBNER. KINDLE EDITION.

---

At the time the razor snare came for Police the Police and Free Thought Project, they had 1.9 million and 3.1 million likes respectively. Both pages were taken down at the same time, and they were removed from Facebook and Twitter on the same day, October 11, 2018. It is possibly the first coordinated social media deplatform operation and was perhaps a blueprint for subsequent actions.

Most of the mainstream media reports on the action simply parroted the reason espoused by Facebook, their now well worn catch-all "Inauthentic Behaviour". From the moment I heard that phrase I thought it sounded distinctly Maoist. The only media outlet to contact the page owners was Rolling Stone, who interviewed them for their "Who Will Fix Face-book?[6]" article.

The project leads tenaciously continue to relaunch on both Facebook and Twitter. They are currently on version number four. They continue to be deplatformed, but they have also mirrored the tactics outlined in this book to maintain their reach and their continuity between successive iterations on the incumbent tech platforms.

ALEX JONES AND INFOWARS

Perhaps the most widely publicized example of a coordinated and systemic deplatforming initiatives is that of Alex Jones of Infowars.

In this case, the tech platforms moved in concert to deplatform Jones. Google cancelled his Youtube account, Facebook suspended his page with 2.1 million followers, even Spotify joined in, removing all of his podcast episodes from the platform.

All of which, according to Jones, only served to drive more web traffic to his website and the Youtube suspension in particular, drove subscriptions to his mailing list. 5.8 *million subscribers* joined his list within the 48 hours of his Youtube channel being canceled.[7] I find that figure hard to believe, frankly. And with respect to the purported sky-rocketing traffic to his website in response to the deplatforming, I can't corroborate it in any public sources.

The Daily Mail article cited Alexa data, for which I don't have an account. When viewed now via Quantcast we do see an August surge around the time of the deplatforming, which then pulled back to normal over the ensuing weeks and months.

Infowars traffic Jan 2018 to present. Source: Quantcast.

The most significant spike in search engine interest coincides with Jones' appearance on the Joe Rogan show on Feb 27, 2019:

Google trends search queries: Alex Jones

Bear in mind, one of the reasons Jones got on Rogan's show was to talk about his deplatforming. This is a recurring theme in this chapter, that deplatforming initiatives have repercussions in unanticipated directions.

To get a sense of where this search volume is, I ran the term

"Alex Jones" against comparison terms "Brexit" and a control term, "Donald Trump":

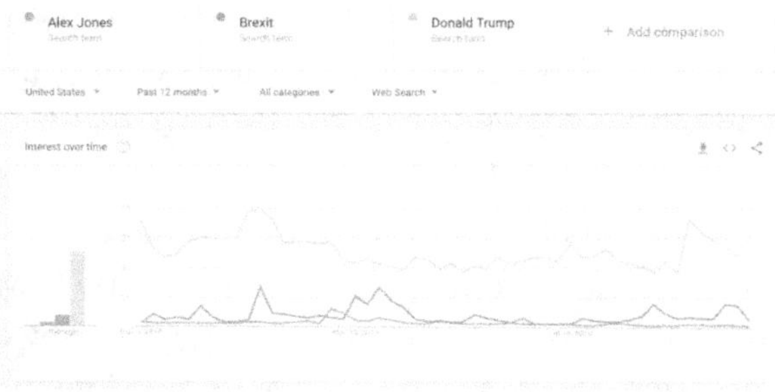

Alex Jones search volume compared to "Brexit" and
"Donald Trump"

The "Alex Jones" search term is in the same ballpark as "Brexit". Granted, it's mostly lower, with occasional spikes above the interest in Brexit on the part of search engine queries.

Overall, the approach Infowars took which enabled them to continue operating largely undaunted agains the headwinds of a global deplatforming attack is straight out of the playbook we recommend in the second half of this book.

## SERIAL KILLER'S SMASH BEST SELLER

Possibly one of the more macabre examples of this dynamic of counter-productivity is the fact that one of the most notorious and reviled predators in the annals of Canadian crime can now count among his accomplishments "best-selling author" as a result of this effect.

Paul Bernardo is currently serving a life sentence for a series of murders and rapes that he and his wife, Karla Homolka, perpetrated in Southwestern Ontario spanning from the late '80s into the early '90s . He has been designated a dangerous offender, which means he will likely never be released.[8]

A close friend of mine was a reporter who covered the trial in 1993-94 and because of the publication ban enacted, was not able to report on most of what he witnessed in court. Much later, he did tell me privately what he learned, and frankly, life in prison seems excessively benign.

Bernardo eventually wrote a novel, "Mad World Order", while in prison and released it in 2015. Apparently it was a spy thriller about a Russian plot to destabilize the West by compromising a next generation social network founded by the novel's protagonist. (As an aside, the fact that the entire post-2016 "Russian meddling" narrative and the Cambridge Analytica scandal was anticipated by, of all people, this guy, is just plain weird.)

At any rate, once the public was onto the fact that this novel existed and was for sale, what followed was inevitable. In Canada, inmates are not legally allowed to profit from their crimes (only career politicians can do that). Had the book been about his own life and crimes, he would not have been able to derive royalties from its sale. But Bernardo didn't do that, thus putting him in a position to profit by the sale of the book.

Outrage followed, which of course catapulted "Mad World Order" to the very top of Amazon's "Movers and Shakers" bestsellers list[9].

Amazon did pull the book, and owing to the fact that the author was already incarcerated with limited ability to take counter-measures, the book does seem dead. It's a rare example that proves the rule. Had Bernardo not been in federal custody for whatever reason, this would have made his career.

WELCOME TO THE WIKI WARS

In 2010, when Wikileaks released information that exposed US wrongdoing in the Middle East, a deplatforming initiative was undertaken. It was informal because there were never any formal charges brought against Wikileaks.[10]

The campaign against Wikileaks was a textbook deplatforming operation:

- Cut off their finances[11]
- Get them kicked off of their hosting[12]
- Have their domain taken down via their DNS provider[13]

All of these actions occurred via behind the scenes pressure on the part of the US government. At no time were formal charges entered against the company, which would have triggered a legal due process. In fact the only legal finding to have ever occurred in connection with the 2010 Wikileaks blockade was when the Icelandic Supreme Court found that Mastercard subsidiary Valitor acted illegally by taking part in blocking donations. They were to be fined 800,000 krona per day (roughly $5,000 USD) if the block was not lifted within 15 days of the ruling. [14]

None of these efforts resulted in a successful suppression of Wikileaks. In fact, given the financial blockade on the part of the global financial network, Wikileaks at that pivotal point in time began accepting an alternative form of donations, via an obscure, emerging digital currency of sorts, called "Bitcoin". At the time of the blockade, Bitcoin was trading at 0.06 USD (6 cents per bitcoin). In 2017 Julian Assange announced[15] that Wikileaks had made greater than 50,000% return on the Bitcoin donations received, and that was when it was trading at around $5,000/each. Over the next year, Bitcoin soared to nearly $19,000 USD and has since pulled back to a range between $8,000 and $10,000. That's still roughly double where it was when Assange talked about it in 2017.

In other words, a concerted, well coordinated deplatforming initiative, executed from within the highest corridors of power with the complicity of the biggest tech companies and financial institutions on earth, not only failed to suppress the whistleblower site, it created an enormous financial windfall for them. Talk about unintended consequences.

## THE SECRET SOCIETY OF SUPER-VILLAINS

Nobody seems to wonder what is supposed to happen to all The Invisibles after they are deplatformed. Inevitably they will start coagulating together in formal or informal networks, on alternative platforms or media outlets.

Answer: Into the Intellectual Dark Web (Cover copyright DC Comics)

Jordan B Peterson went from obscurity to stardom for opposing elements of Canada's proposed Bill C-16. My understanding was that he was specifically against being compelled to use gender neutral pronouns.

This is crucial to understanding the crux of this chapter: it wasn't his stance on the issue, or for that matter, the two books he authored, which catapulted him to stardom. *It was the criticism and the cancel culture that put him there.* Every time there were demonstrations at his public appearances, every hit piece that was published, even the successes in having some appointments or events cancelled, it was all marketing gold for Peterson. It once again demonstrates the dynamic outlined in our aforementioned research paper: boycotts (deplatform attacks) directed against heretofore unknown brands, lift the brand. In this case we can call the brand "JBP".

Given the state of cancel culture today, it was no surprise when Peterson, along with Sam Harris and others, teamed up to launch ThinkSpot. Harris came under fire not for having the wrong views per se, but for having a guest on his podcast who had the wrong views (namely, the social scientist Charles Murray, who researched "the third rail of science": IQ and race).

ThinkSpot[16] is in closed beta and is positioning to be a free speech platform that will monetize creator content, like Patreon, and serve as an alternative social media network to Facebook and Twitter.

## 4CHAN, 8CHAN, ENDLESS CHANS…

There are some places on the internet that are like the back alleys in a bad part of town. What happens to you in there is almost your own fault just for being there.

There is a segment of the internet between the normal web, and the dark web (Onion, Tor) where the terrain is pretty sketchy. Foremost among these are "open message board" sites pioneered by 4chan. Anybody can create a forum within these sites, on any subject matter at all, they are completely unmoderated and pretty well anything goes.

Founded in 2003 by Christopher Poole, 4chan was the original image board having originated as an English version of the Japanese Futaba Channel, a.k.a "2-chan". The latter was primarily focused on manga and anime, which set the tone for 4chan.

Posting to 4chan is anonymous and over time it began to take on wilder and more unhinged characteristics.

Eventually a scandal came along that was too hot even for 4chan. In 2014 all discussion of "Gamergate" was banned on the system after 4chan had somehow become embroiled in the controversy[17].

Because of measures such as this, some thought 4chan to be losing its edge and becoming more authoritarian. Thus in 2013, 8chan came into being, founded by another programmer, Fredrick Brennan. Similar to the famous Spinal Tap metric when it came to Marshall stacks "but these go to 11", 8chan was twice as wild as 4chan.

By 2019, 8chan had become a hotbed of incels, a freshly co-opted Pepe le Frog and on at least two occasions, the forum of choice for mass shooters to post their manifestos before "they went in".

8chan was then deplatformed in August 2018[18], when Cloudflare pulled their services and the site was unsuccessful in finding a new home. As I write this, they have attempted to rise from the ashes as 8kun[19]. The site is still offline given that few service providers want to assume the risk (including us).

Meanwhile, when 8kun relaunched they did it with a dark web version at the same time. That's still up, of course.

Aside from 8chan/8kun, there are a myriad of replacements: Endchan, 7chan, dreamchan, they have now splintered and in my mind have become a phenomenon in itself.

There may as well be a .chan Top Level Domain now. Or maybe "blockchan", where image boards pin their content to widely deployed blockchains which would make them uncensorable and immutable without forking the entire chain or shutting it down entirely. There have been a couple of proof-of-concept projects in this area, but so far nothing has taken off.

The progression of the chan phenomenon shows us another variant from the unintended consequences file.

## AND THEN THERE'S GAB….

Gab[20] arose as a specific reaction to perceived bias against conservatives on the part of the major social media platforms. When anybody right of centre gets kicked off of Twitter, they often end up there.

Facing deplatforming pressures of their own, from having their apps banned from the Apple Store and losing their domain names, Gab has admittedly in my opinion, exacerbated their headwinds through what I've called elsewhere[21], a series of unforced errors.

Despite all that, Gab continues to not only persevere, but grow. Every time somebody is successfully deplatformed from Twitter, you may as well chalk them up as a newly acquired evangelist for Gab.

## PYRRHIC VICTORIES

We've spent this chapter looking at the after-effects of cancel culture to ask if deplatforming attacks actually achieve their stated aims, even when successful.

When a deplatforming succeeds, it may do damage to the primary target in an immediate sense, cutting off their finances, reducing their audience size, and tainting them with pariah status.

Then as the second-order effects unfold, we find that:

- The target garners increased publicity, more brand awareness, possibly *increased* unit sales and more notoriety and word-of-mouth advertising
- Polarity is exacerbated as counter-reactions intensify and siege mentality sets in

- Unanticipated mutations unfold, new configurations emerge, and ascendant technologies are seized upon and harnessed in ways that cannot be fully grasped in the present (Bitcoin, decentralization, the Chans)
- The Invisibles and the canceled gravitate into the Secret Society of Super Villains
- Forbidden streams are driven underground, such as onto the dark web, where they can metastasize into truly unhinged egregores

Regardless of the above, these results won't stop people from trying to press ahead in their attempts at suppression anyway.

So while cancel culture and boycotts may harm individual targets, the larger effect against the ideas and stream of thought they represent is reciprocal.

By way of a thought experiment, what is the current status of Flat Earthers today? Not a lot. Nobody really cares. I've met one in real life. Seems harmless. You see the occasional media piece, and there's that Behind the Curve documentary on Netflix. But there is no effort to deplatform Flat Earthers. If there was, I submit the belief would be spreading like wildfire. Maybe they should start a *fake* deplatforming campaign against themselves to gain more adherents.

The rest of this book is here to give you the tools to defend yourself as much as possible against a deplatforming attack and cancel culture. While nobody can guarantee that you will never be hit with a drawdown to your audience or your business owing to a smear campaign or deplatforming initiative, it doesn't have to be fatal.

Using the approach outlined in this book, you can recover from such an event and come back, perhaps even stronger and louder.

Even if you are not producing heretical content or disagreeing with the herd, you would still do well to read this book if you earn your living online. If the latter is the case, all of this can be read through the lens of disaster recovery and business continuity for your online livelihood.


Let's begin.

## PART II: WHAT YOU DO ABOUT IT_

I disapprove of what you say, but I will defend to the
death your right to say it

- EVELYN BEATRICE HALL

Most actions do not aim at anybody's defeat or loss.
They aim at an improvement in conditions

- LUDWIG VON MISES

How often do you see a business advertising themselves using any of the following:

- Facebook page
- a Youtube channel
- a Twitter handle

Or God forbid...

- A #hashtag?

What about a Medium feed or magazine? Have you ever been handed a business card with a professional's website on it, yet their email address is at some third-party vendor like Gmail or Hotmail? Every time you see this you are witness to an example of "what not to do".

Looking further, what happens too often is that an online venture will pick an external ecosystem to operate on: a Facebook group, a Youtube channel, a Twitter following, etc. They will find their niche, develop a working methodology for building their audience if they are a content creator, or generate leads and sales if they are a business. Things go gangbusters for awhile, and then suddenly (always suddenly), something changes on the selected platform and it's over. It all screeches to halt, on dime, with no warning.

Either the platform changed something that renders your niche in it inoperable, or perhaps your account simply gets closed down. In any case, unless you've planned for this possibility in advance, you're finished.

Australian online entrepreneur James Shramco uses the phrase "Own the Racecourse" .

"The secret to staying power is to own the racecourse. Own the platform that you build your online business on. Own the websites that you publish on. **This puts you in control** and not at the whim of other people and their property."[1]

The way I explain this concept is that whenever you find yourself referring people to your offerings, if the address you give people for that referral (email, URL, etc.) *isn't* under a domain name that *you own or directly control*, then:

A) You are advertising and promoting somebody else's brand, not yours.

·   ·   ·

B) You are probably giving your prospect, lead, customer or user away to some other entity.

Said differently, if your business is called Razorfyre, and you're handing out business cards with razorfyre@gmail.com, or referring people to facebook.com/razorfyre or @razorfyre on Twitter, you really aren't promoting *Razorfyre*. You're actually promoting Gmail, Facebook or Twitter.

Further, all of those followers you have on Twitter or "likes" you have on Facebook, aren't *your* followers or *your* likes. They're Twitter and Facebook's, and they are just allowing you to access those people, for as long as you follow *their* rules and as long as it is in *their* interests to continue to allow it.

The rule of thumb I use is this:

> ***The user / prospect / customer belongs to whomever's database they're in.***
> ***If they aren't in your database, they aren't part of your user base.***

So you've got twelve million Twitter followers? Five hundred thousand Facebook likes? A million viewer Youtube channel? It's all irrelevant. How many of their email addresses do you have? Do you have their billing and contact details? Have you garnered the relevant opt-in permissions to communicate with them? Because at the end of the day, that's what matters the most.

. . .

We'll start with a brief overview on how to own your own race-course, to making sure your online centre of gravity is your own identity and not somebody else's. That gives you the minimum defensive posture from deplatforming attacks and other disasters.

Then we'll spend the remainder of the book refining your defences so that you aren't operating your business or your platform at the whim of arbitrary third-parties.

Finally, we'll circle back to an in-depth look at your online venture's centre-of-gravity, your domain names.

## ALWAYS PROMOTE YOUR OWN BRAND_

You probably already have your own domains and likely have a web presence on them. But too often that isn't your centre of gravity. Too often, people are out there on Twitter, Facebook, Medium or Youtube and building an audience there. That's a mistake.

It may be unavoidable that in order to build up your core following or customer base, you may have to work through these external platforms. But what is required for long term staying power is that you make the mind shift that the audiences or followings you build out there on external platforms are not the end goal. You need to regard them as prospecting tools, lead generators and subscriber magnates.

Don't focus on how many followers, likes or subscribers you have on these external platforms as much as tracking how many of those you need to gain real members of your own community - either via an opt-in to your mailing list, a purchase, a push notification or even a subscription to your RSS feed[1] - anything that puts eyeballs within your direct centre of gravity.

That centre of gravity is, of course, your domain names. Any time you make a reference to some resource that you are making available online, do it via your domain, your web address, never anybody else's.

WHAT THAT MEANS:

Even if you host your email on a third-party provider like Gmail, never hand out your address as at that provider's domain (i.e. razorfyre@gmail.com).

Instead, you setup email forwarding through your domain, razorfyre.com, and you hand out addresses like contact@razorfyre.com that then redirect via email forwarding to razorfyre@gmail.com.

That way if you ever lose access to your account, you don't have to tell all your contacts to change their email address for you, especially if it's to some other platform you don't control. Instead you just update where your email forwarding for razorfyre.com points, and your contacts will not even notice there's been a disruption.

The other part of this would be to have had all of your Gmail account backed up on some other server, again, one under a hostname *you* control (like mailarchive.razorfyre.com) and you still have all your email after your account has been nuked by some external provider.

The principle we discussed above is what we apply across the board:

- Create a resource anywhere
- Reference that resource via a hostname or web address you own and you control
- Keep backups of that resource someplace else

Then, if that resource involves accumulating followers, likes, up votes or any other validation on an external platform, the next component is:

- Build your strategy around cultivating those external validators and converting them into directly contactable users within your own database

Having said that, we're still not done.

It won't do to build out your systems and processes to steadily convert external followers into internal users under your own domain, only to have your domain registrar come along and shut the entire thing down on you.

The final piece of this is to know and understand all the weak points your domains themselves have, and mitigate against them.

Because that part of the equation verges far into the technical, we'll park the domain names for now and suffice it to say, the goal is to build *everything* possible in your online ventures around domain names that *you* own and control. We'll come back to the technical details of securing said domains after we step through each critical component of the rest of your online platform.

Your websites should contain copies and archives of every single piece of content you produce anywhere else on the internet. If you have a Youtube channel, you have copies of every video available on your website. Better still, you would only use Youtube for partial videos, and then pull the user back to your website for the complete version.

Let's take an example of a video where you're interviewing somebody or providing a tutorial and that video is 30 minutes long. Post the first 15 minutes to Youtube. At the end of the first half of that interview you direct viewers back to the rest of the episode, which is hosted on your own website.

If somebody watches that far in, they're interested, and are more likely to follow you back to your home base than if you try this 1 minute in.

Once you have the viewer on your website, you have the opportunity to use a subscriber magnet to get them into your database. You also have a better position to influence what that viewer does next.

Contrast that with Youtube. On Youtube after the video ends they'll tease the viewer with other content that *their algorithm* selects, based on data they've mined from that viewer.

Because you've managed to bring them back to your website, you can suggest *your* related material in front of that viewer instead.

Again, similar to our earlier example of email forwarding at your own domain, this is the basic model we use everywhere: use somebody else's platform to cultivate readers, viewers and generate leads within *your own* ecosystem.

All social media ads, all tweets, any teasers you put out across all social media platforms should be focused on bringing people back to resources under your domains. We put teasers out on all those platforms to be visible for users who commence their searches on those platforms, and who see material shared with them by their connections there.

## CONTENT MANAGEMENT SYSTEMS (CMS)

Many non-technical content producers are lured into putting their trust into external providers because of the ease-of-use for managing their content and getting their web pages, sites and blogs up and running.

What you may not realize is that there is a plethora of options to self-host your own Content Management Systems which makes it just as easy, and in some cases I find, even easier, to produce and publish your own content.

Such systems include Wordpress[1] and Drupal[2]. I've used both. If you're a non-technical user I would recommend Wordpress. It also happens to be the most popular CMS in use across the internet at this time. That ubiquity affords certain advantages:

- Most web hosting providers support it
- There are many freelancers available who you can hire to support and work on it
- There is a a huge ecosystem of developers creating

add-on plugins for all possible functions including:
ecommerce, syndication, media management,
discussions, third-party integrations, etc.
- It's portable: for our purposes this is important. You
can move a Wordpress website from one host to
another without being locked in.

We should speak of the main disadvantage to using Wordpress:
security. Because of the wide range of third-party plugins that
make the ecosystem so flexible and vibrant, the downside is
each plugin can introduce security vulnerabilities.

In order to make Wordpress safe, you therefore *must*:

- Keep your wp-core updated to the current version.
This can be automatically enabled.
- Maintain every single plugin to the most recent
version.
- Keep an offsite backup of the site and data.
- Use a Wordpress Web Application Firewall (WAF)
like Blogvault or Wordfence

Many web hosting providers even have meta builders in their
web hosting dashboards that make it easy to install the Content
Management System so you don't even need to know how to do
that.

(At easyDNS we offer a managed Wordpress platform
called easyPress, that includes setup and installation of Wordpress, automatic updates of the wp-core, and it comes with
Blogvault included, which is a commercial grade Wordpress
backup integration and a Web Application Firewall. )

Blogs are really just a certain variation of website, but I will treat them separately here because a lot of content providers, especially those who produce heterodox material, seem to have an affinity for using third-party blogging platforms like Google's Blogger, Typepad, Tumblr or the *hosted* Wordpress blog (as distinct from the self-hosted Wordpress content management system described in the previous section).

The Wordpress hosted blogs have URLs like:

**razorfyre.wordpress.com**

and it sits on Wordpress servers. On Google it's Blogger, which have URLs that look like

**razorfyre.blogspot.com.**

In any case like these (typepad.com, Tumblr, Myspace) they all pose the same problem for you.

The problem is that you're sitting on somebody else's domain name, and (this is important) you are not only subject to their rules, in the form of their Terms of Service, you are at the mercy of their *whims*. It means their selective, biased or very loosely stated *rationalizations* of their rules carry power over your content.

Even if you are not publishing controversial or heterodox material, you are often granting vast, sweeping rights to the platform host, rights which can even survive past the point where you no longer host your content there.

For example, in Google's Terms of Service, under the "Your Content in Our Services"[1] section:

---

When you upload, submit, store, send or receive content to or through our Services, **you give Google (and those we work with) a worldwide license to use, host, store, reproduce, modify, create derivative works** (such as those resulting from translations, adaptations or other changes we make so that your content works better with our Services), **communicate, publish, publicly perform, publicly display and distribute such content.** The rights you grant in this license are for the limited purpose of operating, promoting, and improving our Services, and to develop new ones. **This license continues even if you stop using our Services** (for example, for a business listing you have added to Google Maps).

---

It's important to point out that in this paragraph the words within parentheses which read like they are limiting the scope of the rights you are granting, are merely *examples* of benign uses that are not actually, legally, limiting the scope of the rights you granted. Said differently, "such as" doesn't mean "limited to".

The one sentence that does seem to limit the scope of the

rights granted, when you read it, "You grant this license for the limited purpose of enhancing the operations of Google", doesn't really limit the scope at all. "Enhancing the operations of Google" can mean anything . It means that they can do whatever they want with your content that serves their purposes.

## REPOSITIONING THIRD-PARTY HOSTED CONTENT

If you are using these third-party platforms for your blog and you don't know what to do in order to move all your content under your own domain, you can take this in stages. You can leave your content on Blogger or Wordpress for now, but what you do as soon as possible is you switch from using their domain to using your domain.

Most of these platforms have the capability to use their system with what is often called "a custom domain". That means a domain you own, that you configure to work with their system. Somewhere there should exist help docs to step you through the process:

**Blogger:**
Setup a Custom Domain
https://support.google.com/blogger/answer/1233387

We have one that specifically walks you through hooking up a domain managed at easyDNS with Blogger:
https://kb.easydns.com/knowledge/connecting-your-domain-to-your-bloggerblogspot/

---

**Wordpress:**

Domains Support
https://en.support.wordpress.com/domains/

---

**Tumblr:**

Custom Domains
https://tumblr.zendesk.com/hc/en-us/articles/231256548-Custom-domains

---

**Typepad:**

Domain Registration and Mapping
https://help.typepad.com/domain_mapping.html

Regardless of which external platform you use, or which registrar you obtain your domain from (although there's a coupon at the end of this book if you want to use easyDNS), the process of switching a third-party content platform over to your own domain involves two phases:

1) Setting up the content host side to recognize requests for your domain as destined for your blog, and

2) Configuring your DNS provider or registrar to route traffic for your domain to your content platform.

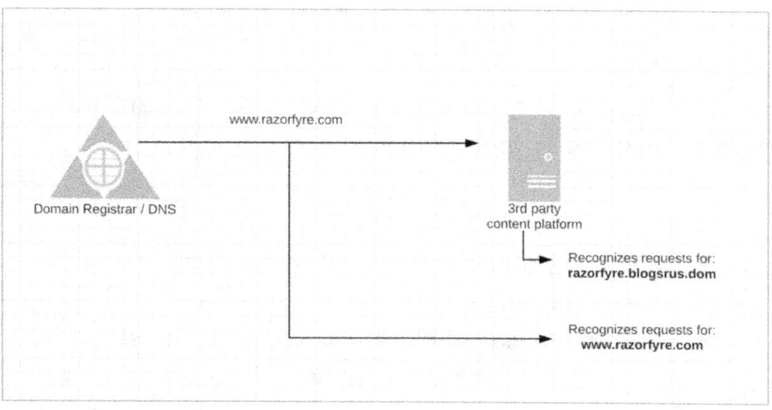


But to fully shift your content and your control over to your own centre of gravity is more of a 6 point plan, of which the process above is simply the first step. We'll walk through the complete process of securing your content under your own domain in as generic terms possible below.

**Step 1: Switch to your own domain for the third-party site**

As outlined above, you register a new domain or use an existing domain that you own. Set that domain up to reference your content on the third-party site. Now instead of referencing your content using links under .blogspot.com or .wordpress.com you are using your own domain.

**Step 2: Back up your content**

Get a copy of all your content from the third-party platform and keep it somewhere under your direct control. I like to use a combination of cloud backup providers (at easyDNS we have easyBackup.com ) and high density storage devices at home and my office.

Each third-party platform should have mechanisms that enable you to get a dump of all your content:

- **Blogger:** https://support.google.com/blogger/answer/41387?hl=en
- **Tumblr:** https://tumblr.zendesk.com/hc/en-us/articles/360005118894-Export-your-blog
- **Typepad:** https://help.typepad.com/back_up.html
- **Wordpress:** https://en.support.wordpress.com/export/*

*(This is for blogs hosted on wordpress.com, for your own self-hosted Wordpress you would use a plugin such as Blogvault, or Wordpress's own Vaultpress)*

Create a process to maintain this backup as you add new content. You could even set up a self-hosted Wordpress blog somewhere and use its importer tool, described below, to import your content from these third-party services.

**Step 3: Set up your own blog on your own hosting provider**

Set up a new blog at your selected hosting provider, under your own domain. From here we're going to do things in a way where even if this new provider deplatforms your site, you'll be able to get back up and running elsewhere without losing any of your content.

**Step 4: Migrate your data**

Import your data into your new blog. If you end up using Wordpress, it comes with several import functions already built-in, just log into your **/wp-admin** and click on the **Tools -> Import** menu options:

As we can see here, Wordpress can import directly from Blogger, Typepad, Tumblr or another Wordpress blog, among others.

**Step 5: Switch your domain to the new host**

This is the cutover moment when traffic destined for your website hosted on the third-party blogging platform will stop going there and instead hit your new blog on your own domain under your control.

There are various ways to do this, and since I'm a DNS and domain guy by profession, I run a real risk here of delving too deeply into the ins-and-outs of the various methods of doing this. In broad terms we can:

1) switch the nameservers to those of your new web host (not preferred)

2) use the nameservers at a DNS service you control to send the traffic to your new site (preferred method).

---

Why is the second method preferred? Is it because I own a DNS company and want to drum up business? Only partially. The main reason is because if you're trying to mitigate against possible deplatforming attacks, you want to keep as much control as possible over all aspects of your domain. When you defer to your web host's nameservers, you are giving up some of that control.

## Step 6: Deeplinks and pointers

Now that the traffic is hitting your new blog with all your old content on your own site and domain, if you started out from **yourwebsite.blogspot.com** and there are still third-party links on the internet out to your old blog, it would be a shame to lose those links and that traffic, not to mention any page relevance ascribed to it by the search engines.

This isn't as easy to do as when you are moving between domains that you control. You're trying to preserve backlinks and search engine relevance from links to your content from a URL you don't control.

## Redirects: Meta Refresh Method

With systems like Blogger, you can edit your page template, and insert some HTML code that will "refresh" the page when somebody lands, and send them to your new blog. In a system like Blogger, or any other third-party blogging platform that enables you to edit your overall template across your entire site, you would enter something like this:

Given razorfyre.blogspot.com wants to get everybody headed to that old URL to the new blog at razorfyre.com, *with* a 301 redirect so that search engines assign page rank to the new link, add the following:

<meta http-equiv="refresh" content="0;url=http://razorfyre.com/" />

At the time of writing, I have disccovered that when you change from a blogspot.com subdomain address to a custom address, and then move that custom domain elsewhere, Blogger will put in a redirect, which is nice, but the way it's implemented is not optimal:

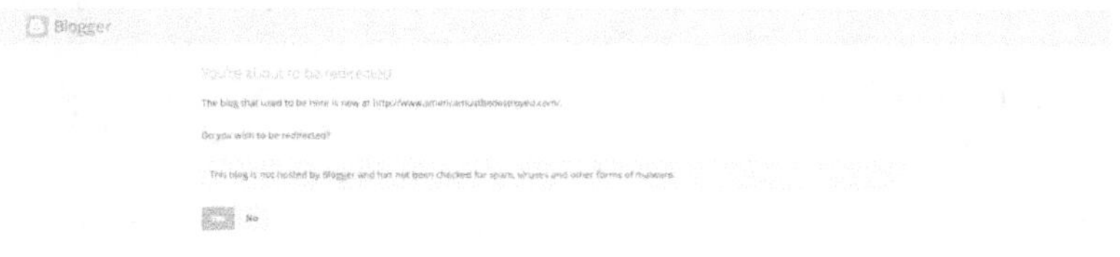


We'd prefer the redirect to be automatic, without requiring a user to click. The wording that the external site has *"not been checked for spam, viruses and other forms of malware"* is also somewhat offputting and may decrease the clickthrough rate.

### Redirects: .htaccess Method

If you are working with a system that gives you access to an **.htaccess** file, like when you are hosted on Wordpress.com, because Wordpress relies heavily on that file, then there is a far better way to redirect to your new site.

· · ·

The ideal way to transition from the old address to your new address would accomplish two things:

1) It uses something called a "301 redirect", because this tells search engines to take any relevance that they ascribe to the old, outgoing URL, and ascribe it to your new page, and

2) It would ideally preserve "deep links", so that for example:

*http://razorfyre.wordpress.com/posts/the_world_is_not_flat.html*

Would 301 redirect to:

*https://razorfyre.com/posts/the_world_is_not_flat.html*

You would accomplish this by placing the following in your web server's **.htaccess** file for your site:

```
RewriteEngine on
RewriteCond %{HTTP_HOST} ^razorfyre.wordpress.com
    [NC,OR]
RewriteRule ^(.*)$ https://razorfyre.com/$1 [L,R=301,NC]
```

If you have a lot of content on the old blog on your third-party platform, it's not a trivial undertaking. You have to decide whether it's worth expending the effort now to be in position to preserve your content later.

Even if you are not at risk of a deplatforming attack, this is the way you *should* be positioning *your* content. On *your* domain. Not somebody else's. Do it this way, as described in the prior section, for any new blogs you create on a go-forward basis so that you can save yourself the hassle of the migration process we outlined in this section.

I wouldn't have thought to include a section on discussion forums were it not for the fact that I constantly bug one of my favourite podcasters to move his insider discussion forum from a Facebook secret group to some other venue under his direct control.

My fear is that the group will eventually be shut down by Facebook. It's true that this personality already has all the email addresses of every member of his group. We have repeatedly emphasized, that is rule #1: You can't consider a user your user until you have their contact info in your database.

While the group would be considered conservative (libertarian, to be exact), it is non-controversial and benign. But in practical terms, anything on the wrong end of the prevailing political spectrum is at-risk. It could be as simple as a low-level functionary in Facebook's community standards group getting a message from some comrade in a militant cell at the other end of the political spectrum and then, with the push of a button, it's all over...

The problem is that it is very tempting to simply leverage the Facebook platform, or others like it, to create your own discussion forums. All the heavy lifting is done, and the odds are high that most of your prospective users are already on Facebook, so the barrier to joining your group is all but removed.

It's another good microcosm of the trade-offs we face toward our entire philosophy of being content creators. There are all kinds low hanging fruit across our entire enterprise: point-and-click discussion groups, blog hosting, email lists, podcast platform, even monetization.

At the risk of overemphasizing the core theme of this book, when you avail yourself of all these easy external platforms to run your content business, after a while it suddenly doesn't look like *your* business anymore. Not after you enumerate all the external vendors whose whims you are now subject to.

It's a longer, harder path toward building your audience on your own terms using assets you control. This particular area of discussion forums is the one application where the added difficulty in doing it this way becomes readily apparent.

It is also, however, one of the areas where perseverance pays off, and your users will be better of for it.

Those benefits include:

- Keep even better security by requiring logins to access the group, and you can optionally make some areas, like a general welcome forum, open to all so prospects can get some idea of the community.
- Many boards support single-sign-on services, so you could enable Facebook logins and dramatically lower the bar for new users to create their own account. Just be sure to configure your systems to take a copy of the remote authenticator userid and create an account locally, as opposed to authenticating against the remote service. In the latter case your users will be frozen out of your forum if their account is terminated on the authentication supplier's platform.
- Archives and threads. This is one area where Facebook is at a pronounced disadvantage. They don't make it easy to find older threads and search archives. You have the option to do that. Further, you can achieve significant long-tail search engine visibility by allowing select channels within your forums to be indexed by search spiders.

There is another consideration here which in my experience is germane to discussion forums in particular. Once you have a discussion forum up and running, and you've successfully pulled in a community of contributors and participants which actually becomes a vibrant, self-perpetuating board, it is effectively too late to change your mind and move it.

I've seen it happen repeatedly, it's happened to me more than once: if you have a successful community going, moving it, or switching it to a different platform is often the kiss-of-death. There are multiple reasons why this tends to be the case, suffice it to say, in the area of discussion boards specifically, whatever decision you make when you're starting out to create one, you will more or less be stuck with it for the duration.


## COMMENT MANAGEMENT

This is the other aspect to online discussion. Again we find low-hanging fruit like embedded Facebook commenting, or specialized firms like Disqus, that make it easy to add commenting and discussion to your blog posts, etc. Once again, however, using a third-party comment management system leaves you vulnerable to having somebody else decide what can or cannot be said, even if you are using your own website or blog.

Facebook's embedded comment box is, of course, subject to the usual Facebook's notoriously capricious interpretation of their community standards.

Disqus has been also known to pull the plug when somebody colours outside the lines.[1] If you simply search on "Disqus censorship", there are myriad complaints of comments from one side of the political spectrum being marked as spam or hidden without the site owners being aware or having any control over it. There was even a report of Disqus inserting affiliate links into client blogs[2], which was called a bug when reported, but serves to illustrate our point. You are permitting an external entity to manipulate content on your site.

Comments reside in the Disqus database, where posters and user profiles could be cross-referenced with their activity on other sites entirely.

There are options to sync your Disqus comments locally with your own database, and if you're using this system you most definitely should be doing that at the very least. However, in my research on Disqus, I found some complaints about certain comments were being dropped down the rabbit hole, and they weren't being synced locally either.

Of course, you're not exposed to that kind of risk if you just make sure you keep as many facets of your online activities under your own umbrella.

To that end, here are come options for self-hosting your own comments / discussion forums:

## SELF-HOSTED DISCUSSION OPTIONS:

**XenForo** https://xenforo.com/

We use this one for our customer support forums on our Zoneedit subsidiary. It works great and has a pleasing aesthetic layout. It natively supports login via Facebook, Google or Twitter.

Naturally, I advise all end-users against becoming reliant on using their social media accounts for single-sign-on (SSO) because, when your social media account gets nuked, you will be locked out of all those websites.

(Some websites that use Facebook or Google for logins create a copy account from information supplied via an initial request to the external system's authentication protocol. This is preferred. In most cases the client websites simply always use the external Single Sign-On protocol on every login. For example, my Spotify account is tied to my Facebook account. If Facebook terminates your account, you lose access to all services that key on it for logins.)

But it can be handy to make it easy for your users to easily begin participating in your forum without having to create a new account. This is why I'd advise my podcaster personality above to consider an option like this one, because that way all of his existing secret Facebook group members would be able to easily get started in a forum like this.

**vBulletin** https://vbulletin.com

This is one of the longest running options in existence and

vBulletin powers some *huge* discussion forums. It also has additional components that you can plug in such as a blogging platform that would enable your board members to run a blog on the forum.

There is also a cloud hosted version (which I always have an aversion to - again, it's on their system, not yours).

**InvisionBB** https://invisioncommunity.com/

Another long running player in the space that I've used in the past and been satisfied with is InvisionBB, which is now part of a larger community platform that encompasses file sharing, blogging, ecommerce, calendars and a CMS.

Again, Invision has moved toward cloud hosting like everybody else, but they still do fully support on premise hosting, which is what I recommend.

These systems all support multimedia types, markdown language and the same level of interactivity and inter-member messaging as Facebook.

## CAVEATS OF SELF-HOSTING YOUR FORUMS

The options I outlined above are all commercial grade, they are not free. There are numerous free forum software packages out there, but the target audience of this book is serious content creators who derive a living online. If that is what you're doing then use commercial grade gear to run your operation, it's just a cost of doing business. When you use commercial, even if open source, instead of free packages, you are getting professionally coded and - more importantly - supported software.

Security vulnerabilities are a constant reality of the online space. With paid packages you can expect immediate notifications, followed by patches and updates when security issues become known. With free packages, the open source community often will patch something fast, but generally the onus is on *you* to keep track of issues, make sure your installation is always up to date and maintain with patches. I just find that as a general tendency, when using free packages it just tends not to get done.

As I stress above, I prefer on-premise self-hosting of these types of components, but that may not be for everybody. My aversion to cloud hosted options aside, you at least offload the upgrades and security patches to the vendor and it still is, technically *your* data, *your* instance. You either need to be technically competent yourself, or have people on your staff or at your disposal whose job it is to run this stuff.

If you do opt for cloud versions of these packages, or any other types of systems we cover, always look for a vendor that has some data export, offsite backup functionality. Then make it one of your first orders of business when getting set up with one to put in place an automated process that will export and back up your data on a regular basis. See the section on **Backing It All Up** later in this book.

An overall email strategy includes the following components:

- Your organizational email ( you@razorfyre.com )
- Your email marketing list and automation management
- Broadcasting email to your list

## YOUR ORGANIZATIONAL EMAIL

This component may not seem directly relevant to your content publishing endeavours. However, the number of mailing lists and newsletters I subscribe to where the list owner is using an email address at some third-party provider, or worse, a *free* third-party email provider, never fails to astound me.

Recall our mantra, if the user is not in your database then it's not really your user. Similarly, if your personal and company email address is not under a domain name that you own and directly control, *then it's not really your email* either.

Think about that - all of those messages you're sending back and forth, to prospects, to sources, to *confidential* sources, if you're doing that from a Gmail or an Hotmail address then it isn't really your email correspondence, it's Google's, or it's Microsoft's. You have no expectation of privacy, and as I've documented frequently over the years of #AxisOfEasy[1] (our free weekly newsletter covering privacy and security issues), your third-party email communications are routinely parsed, scanned and analyzed by numerous providers.

Your email should be under your own domain name, full stop. ALWAYS do this. Never not do this.

Not only are your communications not private when you use third-party email addresses, but you are unwittingly putting more of your online existence under control of other people and increasing the damage of being deplatformed.

How often is your email address your login username, not only with your email provider but with all other online platforms and services upon which you rely? Now think about your email provider deciding they don't like your skepticism of anthropogenic global warming and they decide to terminate your account for being "hateful". Not only have you been locked out of your own email, you are now also locked out of every other online system where you used that email as a login id. ( This same vulnerability applies when you use your Facebook or Twitter login for other systems we talked about in the previous chapter. )

---

The bare minimum then, is that your email address for yourself and your business, company, organization, etc., is under a domain name that you own and you control. You may still be on a third-party vendor if you do this but you do not run your own mail server. When you buy your Domain from your web host or domain registrar and set it up with email hosting, you are running your email from your own domain, but you're doing it atop your provider's infrastructure. Just always bear in mind the reality that all of your providers are in a position to screw you.

Thus the same trade-offs apply that we come across repeatedly in this book (and will again below, when we look at email automation options). You're theoretically at risk when you use a cloud hosting solution or managed provider, but you can mitigate that risk by using your own domain that you control. That way if you do encounter difficulties with your provider, you have options. You can switch away to another provider or bring the functionality in-house.

It's no different for email. You can go a step further and run your own mailserver. With email you can even do both. I host my own email under my domains at my domain provider (ok, I run the company so there's that). But I also have a third-party, completely unrelated mail server set up that gets a copy of every single email I send or receive. It just sits there, firewalled off from the world, archiving *everything*. If one day I get ousted by the board and they have security escort me off the premises, I have a copy of all my emails, and a stand-by server that I could simply switch to being my main mail hub with a simple DNS update.

If you're using Gmail, or Hotmail or any other email address where the part after the @ isn't a domain you own, stop doing that right away. That's your first order of business in taking control over your online presence.

*(The one possible exception I can think of are reporters who use*

*encrypted email services like Protonmail or Tutanota. In that posi-tion, I would still use that for communications with sources and have my main email running under my own domain. You can use GPG encryption with your own email.).*

## YOUR EMAIL MARKETING LIST AND AUTOMATION MANAGEMENT

The most important component of your online platform is your email list. If you don't have your user's, customer's, viewer's, member's email, then they are *not your* user, customer, viewer or member. They belong to whomever has their email address in their database.

We cannot overemphasize this point, borrowed from the Bitcoin mantra of "not your keys, not your coins":

**The user belongs to whomever's database they're in. If you don't have their contact details in your database, then you can't think of them as part of your user base. At best, they are a lead or a prospect.**

When you *do* have your email list, you can use that to rebuild from any setback.

There is a parable, possibly apocryphal, since I am having diffi-culties sourcing it (my recollection was that I originally heard it in a Brian Tracy audiobook), about the oil magnate John D. Rockefeller. When he testified in the Standard Oil anti-trust proceedings in the late 1800s, he told the assembled court that if he were to lose his entire company, the oil, the money, the pipelines, everything, yet be allowed to keep his people and his organization, he would be able to rebuild his entire enterprise within four years.

Today, that's your list. With your list you can rebuild anything the social justice warriors tear down and you can probably do it faster than your prior iterations.

EMAIL LIST MANAGEMENT

However, while having your email list is the major component, it's just one part of it.

You still need to be able to send email to your list, and believe it or not, some of the services that exist to facilitate this have been known to actively censor the content of your email messages to your own mail list:

## Digital marketer Mailchimp bans anti-vaccination content

The move to block vaccine misinformation follows similar actions by other tech companies including Facebook and Amazon.

June 17, 2019, 11:46 AM EDT

By Brandy Zadrozny

Digital marketer Mailchimp has removed several anti-vaccination activists from its platform and will no longer provide services to newsletters that push anti-vaccination content.

The move to block the anti-vaccination rhetoric follows similar actions by other tech companies and comes on the heels of increased pressure from public health advocates and lawmakers on digital platforms to curtail the spread of health misinformation.

In the screen grab above, the mail service Mailchimp starting blocking people from sending messages containing so-called "anti-vaxxer" content and went so far as to remove accounts from their system for sending messages deemed to be misinformation.

What you or I believe about vaccinations is immaterial. In

my mind, it is indefensible for an infrastructure provider to make *any* subjective opinion about the content of its downstream, paying customers. The only thing an email service should concern itself with is whether the recipient list is clean, that their user is not spamming anybody, and that the content being sent is virus free. That's it.

What's in the messages shouldn't be anybody's business other than the sender and the recipients, those people who have actually opted-in to the list.

Alas, increasingly this is not the world we live in. Service providers seem to think it's ok to increasingly moderate the content of their customers, and all this looks to get worse before it gets better.

We've used Mailchimp in the past and probably still have the odd autoresponder or automation with them. At easyDNS we use Klaviyo, ActiveCampaign and Aweber.

These are all centralized solutions which today are more than adequate for our requirements. But they would all be in a position to pull the same stunt as Mailchimp and start enforcing their own subjective preferences on customers' content.

Again, we have another situation where if you find yourself running into a scenario where your email broadcast service is censoring your content, you can switch to a self-hosted email marketing suite. There are numerous options with varying levels of sophistication, ranging from free and open source, to paid commercial packages.

## Self-Hosted Email Managers

Some self-hosted systems are built to run atop of a specific provider. For example, Sendy[2], a commercial system (one-time

$59 license) specifically works with Amazon SES[3] (Simple Email Service). Not my first choice because then we're stuck operating at the whim of Amazon.

Ideally, we want a system that is provider agnostic. That means it doesn't care how you are actually sending the email, it is either doing it itself, directly sending the email from the server it's hosted on, or it's relaying through a third-party sender, but one that can you can switch away from if you have problems.

One example is Maudic[4], which is a free, open source package, which also has a cloud hosted version. It supports segments, bounce handling and has plugins to integrate with numerous systems and CRMs like SugarCRM, Hubspot, Salesforce, Citrix, Outlook and Twitter.

We used to use Interspire Internet Email Marketer for our Zoneedit subsidiary, but they've since sunsetted that suite. But I mention it to make a point: as with any self-hosted suite, you *must* keep it up to date with the most current version. Interspire's package had some software vulnerabilities and on two separate occasions (years apart), an intruder gained access to our instance and sent spam emails to the customer lists we had stored in the system. It was very embarrassing.[5]

This article[6] lists seven self-hosted packages including the mentioned above.

DELIVERABILITY CONSIDERATIONS WHILE SELF-HOSTING

When self-hosting your email you have complete control over what goes into the content of your broadcasts, not to mention the responsibility to ensure that they contain no viruses and are not spam.

All recipients should be opt-in and preferably, opt-in and confirmed.

If you are lax in this regard you will find your IP space being penalized with a poor sender reputation, and that will diminish your deliverability rates. Even if your email does get through, they may be sent straight to your recipients junk folder.

There are several things you, or your techies, can do to improve this situation, including:

- Publishing Sender Policy Framework (SPF) data on your domain
- Employing Domain Keys Identified Mail (DKIM), and
- Using Domain-based Authentication and Conformance (DMARC)

It may be slightly outside the scope of this book to delve into the gory technical details of these mechanisms, but we can outline their functions and behaviours here. We'll supply a few pointers to get your tech personal started, if they don't already know this (I vaguely remember some guy wrote an obscure DNS book that has an entire section on this stuff).

**Sender Policy Framework (SPF)**

"SPF publicly broadcasts which mailserver hosts are allowed to originate (or relay) email for a specified domain."[7]

By telling the world which servers and networks are legitimately originating email from your domain name, you are explicitly disavowing spam, phishes or what are euphemistically called "Joe jobs".

In our context this has additional relevance as one of the

tactics your ideological opponents may use as part of a deplatforming campaign is to send out fake emails purporting to be from you, containing content that reflects poorly on you.

The project overview for SPF is at http://www.open-spf.org/

And we have an online wizard that enables you to create your SPF records here: https://spfwizard.com

## Domain Keys Identified Mail (DKIM)

While SPF advertises *who* can legitimately originate or relay email purporting to be from your domain, DKIM provides a mechanism to validate the content of the messages themselves.

Using DKIM, a recipient can know that the message they are reading is the same as the message that was sent and that it has not been altered in any way in transit.

*(The way Simple Mail Transport Protocol, SMTP, works, an email message may hop across any number of servers between the point of origin and ultimate recipient. At any point in that journey, anybody with admin level access to an intermediary host has the ability to alter the messages in transit).*

Like SPF, the DKIM public data is published via a TXT record in your domain's DNS. However DKIM also requires an extra procedure in that your originating mail server must also have your domain's public DKIM keys installed, so that it can cryptographically sign your messages as they are sent.

An interesting point of fact is that when the now infamous Podesta emails were leaked in the run-up to the 2016 US election, initial claims that some of the more damaging messages were forgeries were quickly discredited by the fact that the emails were DKIM signed.[8]

See more on DKIM at the https://dkim.org project site.

·  ·  ·

## Domain-based Authentication and Conformance (DMARC)

You would not use DMARC in isolation. It's something you put in place on top of DKIM and SPF. Once you have asserted which internet hosts can originate your domains email (SPF) and you are signing said messages (DKIM), DMARC provides a framework to describe what should happen next should a mail server receive an email that fails these checks.

In addition to instructing mail servers how to handle failures, DMARC provides a reporting mechanism so that you can see what kinds of failures are occurring. This will give you warning that some kind of attack or event is in progress.

You can read an overview of DMARC at the project home page: https://dmarc.org/

The theory is that by implementing these mechanisms you will improve email deliverability. It signals to the network that as a mail host and originator, you know the rules and are playing by them.

We still see cases reported of large email carriers sending messages from smaller players to the spam folder despite the presence of these mechanisms. One of the reasons is that you are still heavily impacted by the IP reputations of who your neighbours are on the network. If your hosting provider is lax on spam and has an overall network reputation to reflect that, it will impact you regardless of what measures you implement.

You can mitigate this by running your self-hosted email automation suite on a server you control and they have it relay the broadcasts through a well known transactional email sender.

Third-party senders include industrial strength systems like Mailgun[9], Sendgrid[10] or Postageapp[11], or even a raw outbound relay like my own firm's easySMTP outbound relay[12].

## BROADCASTING EMAIL TO YOUR LIST

In the case of all centralized solutions like Aweber, Klaviyo, et al. they will also handle the broadcast function of actually sending the email messages to your list. For this reason, these services have *some* cover when they assert control over who you're emailing, and to some extent *what* you're emailing them, because it's their IP addresses which will be penalized and blacklisted if they're found to be originating spam, or worse, viruses.

But if you end up going with a self-hosted option, you have to decide whether to have your server instance itself send the email broadcasts to your list, or whether to use yet another third-party provider to do it.

In the case of broadcast emails, using a third party provider can make sense, because most of them have built up clean reputations on the internet, in the sense that their IP address net blocks are known. They have generally reliable reputation scores and thus have higher deliverability rates to major providers.

If you're running a self-hosted system on some IP you just put live, that can be seen as lower quality with a lower reputation, because the major email hubs have not seen traffic from it in the past and may score it lower in their spam filters. Worse, there is the possibility that the IP you've inherited to run your self-run instance on was previously used by a bad actor and has really earned a poor reputation.

## PODCASTING_

We can treat podcasting in the same manner we do videos. The low hanging fruit is to post them on iTunes, Spotify and Youtube. But then you run the risk of those platforms deciding your content is problematic and jettisoning you.

Both iTunes and Spotify removed Alex Jones' podcasts.[1] It's immaterial what you think of Jones (I've never seen a single episode) the precedent has been set and it'll probably get worse before it gets better.

If your primary content format is podcasts, then I would make it a point to publish via your own website all editions of your work.

From there, put the teaser / "Part I" segments out via iTunes, Spotify, Youtube, etc, then via a call-to-action within the episode and on your accompanying page, pull as many users back to your own website for the remaining piece.


I was a subscriber to Catherine Austin Fitts' Solari Report[2] for a few years, and her podcasts were all premium content. There were no free episodes floating around on Youtube, etc.

Subscribers would have to log in to the Solari website and explicitly download the podcast files. That's a lot higher friction than conventional wisdom would say is feasible, yet she makes it work.

Forum Borealis[3] does a variation of what I suggest, splitting long-form podcast editions into multiple pieces, making the complete episode available to premium subscribers immediately, while putting the the first part up on the major platforms and adding a two week delay for the remaining parts.

Tom Woods and Bob Murphy distribute their Contra Krugman podcast[4] via the major platforms as well as through the up-and-coming challengers, like Stitcher[5]. One minor tweak I would make in the way they do it would be to reverse the order of the available platforms when they announce them: "Subscribe to us on Stitcher or iTunes".

(Or even better, "subscribe to our podcasts via contrakrugman.com/podcasts/ or via your favourite services like Stitcher and iTunes.")

Say them in the order you prefer the most people to use, the objective being to spread the distribution as much as possible away from the 800-pound gorillas and toward the resources you control or the smaller challengers.

This is the lifeblood of your online existence. In the next section, when we look at good revenue models vs bad revenue models, the good ones will circle back here, where you have to be on top of how you receive payments and revenues using payment processors, gateways and integrators.

You don't need to have a merchant credit card account to accept credit card payments online. You can go through aggregators. The most popular ones are Stripe or Paypal. But here again we have the hauntingly similar situation where they are effectively the incumbents of the space. With that size comes the power to deplatform, and they have also been known to jump on the bandwagon when someone gets branded as the latest "Invisible Man", as happened to Wikileaks in 2010 and Alex Jones in 2018.

They also both pulled Gab.ai in response to a mass shooting later that year, which I wrote about at the time on the easyDNS blog.[1] (That post and selected others are included in herein as an appendix.)

We aren't going to cover Stripe or Paypal here. Sure, go

ahead and use them, but be prepared to have a backup payment provider[2] should you come under their ire.

## PAYMENT PROCESSORS / GATEWAYS

These are companies that will process credit card payments on your behalf, in many cases even if you don't have a merchant credit card account of your own.

2Checkout

This one has come a long way over the years and supports all variants of ecommerce, from software-as-a-service / online systems, to storefronts, recurring payments, subscriptions and even manages affiliate programs.

Authorize.net

Has been around forever and almost every payment integration I've come across interfaces with it. They started as a payment gateway, so you would need a merchant account, but then recently added merchant account services too. This makes them an alternative or backup to Stripe. So far I have not heard of any ideologically based deplatformings out of Authorize.net

Other processors I've heard of but don't have any experience with include: Dwolla, Worldpay, Securepay and Braintree.

## PAYMENT INTEGRATIONS

Integrators are ways to bolt into whatever payment processor you are using on the backend. Here the idea is to put as much of your payment collection apparatus under your direct control. You can configure your integrations for multiple payment provider backends, that way you can switch to your backup fairly easily if you have it all set up in advance.[3]

I'll mention two integrations here:

## WooCommerce

This is a payment plug in for Wordpress that does, quite simply, *everything*. It integrates with all the payment gateways. It even has plugins for making calls to couriers like Fedex or Purolator, your post office service, label printing, recurring subscriptions, the works. Since I've been recommending Wordpress as the preferred CMS throughout all this, it makes sense.

## Mals-E Commerce

Here's a shout-out to an independent player who's been around for over twenty years and done a great job evolving with the times and staying current. Mals-E has a free level and can get you up and running with payments in no time.

## ALTERNATIVE PAYMENTS - CRYPTO CURRENCIES

I'm a fan of crypto-currencies such as Bitcoin, Ethereum, Monero, and the like. It's almost as if Bitcoin was created to route around centralized top-down control or something.

It's a no brainer for anybody colouring outside the lines of allowable discourse to be accepting Bitcoin as a payment method. The combination of being outside the control of in-group of the Silicon Valley and Bitcoin's long-term deflationary trend, punctuated by ever increasing super-spikes in value, make it worth your while to simply hang out a shingle that you accept Bitcoin, and then just accumulate it and sit on it for the long haul when you receive any.

It's unlikely that at this stage of adaptation that you will earn enough crypto-currency on a recurring basis to run your operations or derive a living - not unless you are deeply embedded within that ecosystem. However, you can accumulate a decent holding, which may then experience a subsequent appreciation in value which can be cashed out at opportune moments. We've done this ourselves once or twice at easyDNS since we started accepting Bitcoin as a payment method in 2013.

If you are interested in accepting Bitcoin at your business or website and don't know where to start, Tom Woods and Bob Murphy put out a free guide on how to do this easily.

https://tomwoods.lpages.co/how-to-accept-bitcoin/

If your requirements are a little more high end, we're working on a product here at easyDNS designed specifically for businesses who want to integrate Bitcoin payments into their invoicing systems. You can get on the invite list for that at the following URL:

https://easydns.com/landers/earn-crypto/

The three worst revenue models in terms of monetizing your content with an eye toward lowering your susceptibility to deplatforming attacks are as follows:

1. Youtube
2. Google Adsense (Advertising networks)
3. Patreon

Let's take a look at each of these to better understand why. Despite the seeming ease with which one can earn a revenue stream from their content using these systems, by doing so you are existing purely at the whim of external forces outside of your control. (One of the major reasons I personally went into business for myself was to minimize the amount of external control others had over my life. This is a common trait among business owners and solopreneurs. When you come to rely on any of these platforms to earn your livelihood, you are doing the opposite: you are maximizing the control that other people and their political ideology have over you).

YOUTUBE

With Youtube you have all the failings described throughout this book: you don't have the viewers in your database, you can't email them directly. Youtube arbitrarily decides who gets demonetized and nobody readily understands the reasons why.[1]

At the end of the day, if your revenue model is built on Youtube monetization, then you are living entirely at the whim of somebody else's subjective opinion of your content. You are not in control and those millions of viewers are not your customers or users.

Just got deplatformed on YouTube.

My other channels are at risk as well.

No explanation provided by YouTube. No prior strikes or warnings on this channel.

It's getting dicey out there.

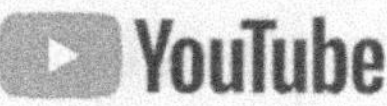


We'd like to inform you that due to repeated or severe violations of our Community Guidelines (https://www.youtube.com/t/community_guidelines) your YouTube account Libertarian Union has been suspended.

After review we determined that activity in your account violated our Community Guidelines, which prohibit spam, scams or commercially deceptive content (https://support.google.com/youtube/answer/2801973?hl=en).

Please be aware that you are prohibited from accessing, possessing or creating any other YouTube accounts. For more information about account terminations and how our Community Guidelines are enforced, please visit our Help Center.

If you would like to appeal the suspension, please submit this form.

Help center · Email options · Report spam

11                                              22 Comments

If you are a Youtube star (a "youtuber" I guess), the best way to think of yourself in order to understand your true position in the world is as a freak show attraction in the circus. You are one of many, you are expendable, and you get fed with chicken scratch from the ringmaster's ticket sales. They will have absolutely no compunction over kicking you to the curb when the blush wears off and the circus leaves town.

## THE CORRECT WAY TO USE YOUTUBE:

We talked about this earlier, but we can cover it a bit more here. It is worth having a presence on Youtube. A certain sub-section of people actually search there first for whatever it is they're looking for. Youtube, like Facebook, Twitter, and the rest, are your tendrils. You have your presence there, people can find you, but your primary objective in being out on those platforms is to pull people back to a place where you are in control and where you can obtain their contact details. You want to make them into your user, customer or viewer.

## GOOGLE ADSENSE

It seemed like an elixir of life when it first came out - add a simple javascript widget to your website, and bingo, start earning money on your content. Over the years I've owned a few side project websites that relied on Adsense for their revenue model. Even without being in any way controversial, I still learned to dread the inevitable notice from Google about some page on one or another of my websites that didn't conform to Adsense policies for whatever reason.

Eventually it got to a point where I got sick of Google dictating what I could and could not do on my own websites, and with CPM rates in what seemed a secular decline anyway, I just removed Adsense from most of my sites.

Today, it's worse. Maybe you're fine with Google Adsense. But these days when other people aren't fine with your content, they will go look at your website and see what kinds of ads are coming up and they will then pressure those advertisers to stop running ads on your site.

Google's Adsense allows advertisers to exclude websites from their ad buys, so when pressured, advertisers often capitulate and add your site to their exclusions. Then they can virtue signal that they're onside with the social justice mob. The Twitter collective Sleeping Giants is known for this.

Founded by ad industry veteran Matt Rivitz, he ran the Sleeping Giants collective anonymously for a year before being outed by the Daily Caller[2].

Running any kind of third party ad network on your site leaves you open to these types of campaigns. In the next section we'll look at sponsorship and ad deals which put you in direct contact with your advertisers and can forge a stronger bond that can withstand a deplatforming attack of this type.

PATREON

Patreon is a service that has taken the world by storm since launching in 2013. Billing itself as a crowdfunding membership platform, it makes it trivially easy for content creators to solicit recurring donations through the platform.

There's only one problem: if Patreon doesn't like your content, they can pull the plug on you. To be more charitable to Patreon, whose CEO claims they do not terminate accounts based on content[3], they can terminate your account at their discretion.

In their deplatorming explainer video[4], Jack Conte describes how Patreon is capable of removing everybody on the abuse team's subjective feelings out of the platform vs. deplatform equation by referring exclusively to...

# Manifest Observable Behavior

Conte explains that this means:

---

"Manifest observable behavior is to remove personal values and beliefs when the team is reviewing content. It's a review method that's entirely based on observable facts: what has a camera seen, what has an audio device recorded. It doesn't matter what your intentions are, your motivations, who you are, your identity, your ideology. The trust and safety team only looks at Manifest Observable Behavior. We get rigorous and specific because we're talking about removing a person's income. The authority to take away a human being's income is a sobering responsibility. It is not something to be done on a whim."

---

He then cites the specific case that when Patreon terminated Defend Europe and Laura Southern, they did so because "they directly obstructed a search and rescue ship in the Mediterranean and made a variety of statements to outline plans to obstruct similar rescue ships in the future".[5]

If you read any of the counter-factuals about this incident, or any deplatforming for that matter, you will see that it may not be as cut and dry as Comte thinks his system makes it. For one, Southern denies that she took part in the event that got her account deplatformed or asserts that she was not there as a participant but as a journalist. Who to believe?

The reality is that nobody can remove their subjectivity from any process that involves a judgement call. A lot of these tech platforms seem to think it's incumbent upon them to judge what is the mind of others, the intent of others, the *possible* outcome of other people's actions. Not to mention that when they do, they are frequently, in essence, adjudicating international law.

Patreon is not alone here by any stretch. Both Twitter and Facebook[6] have policies that they can suspend user accounts (or remove "verified" status in the case of Twitter) based in their activities *off of their respective platforms* including out in the real physical world.[7]

Whenever I think of the logical extensions that would arise in a world where all manner of private entities are taking it upon themselves to render judgement and level sanctions on others, with a complete absence of due process, it reminds me of an old episode of that venerable TV classic, The Simpsons.

In it, the archetypical evil old rich white guy, Montgomery Burns, is being forcibly confined to a mental institution after exhibiting confusion in a supermarket when pondering a bottle of Ketchup (normal) vs one of Catsup (heresy). As the men in white suits are dragging Burns away, the affable Chief Wiggum explains what is happening to him, "Relax. You've gone off your nut, and you're being committed to an insane asylum. *Those grocery store clerks signed the commitment papers*".

Comedy intuits reality. There should be only one authority

empowered to judge and sanction you based on your real world behaviour, and that is the prevailing law of the land. Everything else should be governed by private agreement and contracts between relevant counter-parties.

That means online vendors should merely be posting clear cut terms of service that outline exactly what they will and will not tolerate *on their own platform* and leave it there. That's hard enough to get right. After more than 20 years of overseeing an abuse desk at a service provider like easyDNS, I know.

The saving grace with Patreon is that you get access to your supporters' email addresses, so if you must use it, make sure you are putting those in an off-system database.

## ALTERNATIVES TO PATREON

If you are using Patreon, then you should also be using any alternatives at your disposal to try and spread your supporters across multiple systems.

**SubscribeStar**[8] is a challenger to Patreon. This is where Alex Jones wound up as well as citizen journalist Andy Ngo and Dr. Gad Saad. Say what you will about Jones, nobody's holding a gun to your head to pay attention to or support him. But SubscribeStar is amassing a roster of content creators who are credible, yet the frequent subjects of attack.

SubscribeStar specifically bills itself as:

---

Independent and Flexible
No    big    corp    murky    policies,    no    silly

macromanagement or overreactions, and no judgements or biases whatsoever.

---

Their guidelines[9] are refreshingly clear and unambiguous. I don't like that their default sign-up method is to use your Facebook login. Again, if you do this and Facebook suspends you, it will affect all sites where you use that login. Use the "sign up with your email" option instead.

**BitBacker**[10] is a Bitcoin based system so it can't do recurring monthly payments yet, but it is still good to be accumulating some Bitcoin. If you can afford to just sit on it, you may do well on value appreciation over time if the past few super-spikes are any indicator.

What I like about BitBacker is you enter your own wallet address in your profile and they just send you your BTC. They don't hold your balance in their own wallet within the system, so if BitBacker themselves were to ever disappear, you still have the BTC you earned in your own wallet.

A general principle when putting multiple options in front of people, put the 800-pound gorilla last. You want to spread your users across the challengers as much as possible, and if you're about to convert somebody into a supporter who doesn't have an account on any of these systems yet, they may just go with the first option in the list. So if you put SubscribeStar there first, you can nudge the distribution a tad further away from Patreon, leaving you slightly less exposed to their taking a dim view of your **Manifest Observable Behaviour.**

## A BRIEF ASIDE ABOUT MANIFEST OBSERVABLE BEHAVIOUR

Anecdotally, toward my previous point, at one point none other than Antifa had one of their websites' DNS on easyDNS[11]. They were a customer of a client[12] who specializes in protecting civil society groups and dissident political journalists from persecution and DDoS attacks. We never dealt with them, we always deal with our client.

But sometimes my blood would boil over when I saw incidents in which masked Antifa thugs purportedly assaulted defenceless targets in the streets. When I saw the video of them swarming journalist Andy Ngo, for example,[13] I caught myself thinking "When I get back to my computer I'm booting them the hell off the system".

But I didn't do that. I never do that.

What I do when I catch myself thinking like that, is I force myself to look at the Antifa website (the stuff that we were actually doing the DNS for), and I read over the content.

When I did that it became evident that there was a distinction between what content appears on the website, the part my company was providing infrastructure for, and what takes place out in the streets of Seattle or Portland. What Tom Comte would deem "Manifest Observable Behaviour".

Further, and as I said earlier, it's rarely cut-and-dry in that there are usually counter-narratives to be found. For example, an article in Rolling Stone[14] that paints a different picture that is somewhat orthogonal to my initial impression of the Andy Ngo incident.

So which is it? Did Antifa beat up a defenceless journalist or was it a deliberate provocation and troll?

And that is the entire point: from my vantage point over here as some guy running a tech company, *I don't know*.

Further, even it's the former, then do the perpetrators of that assault transmit culpability to the people writing content for the website? Given that Antifa is a decentralized, cell-based movement, I would have to say it isn't tenable to assert that connection.

All I, or my company, or any company can competently assess, is what happening on our respective systems. Nothing else.

If all this low-hanging fruit is fraught with danger and pitfalls, how is one to monetize their content while still protecting themselves from raving mobs of high-minded puritans?

By all means, you can use the aforementioned methods once you're aware of the weaknesses and how to reduce vulnerability. As a general practice, spread your eggs across multiple baskets and try not to let yourself get into a position of being overly reliant on a single source of revenue.

But to really take things into your own hands and control your destiny, it usually means cutting out the middle-men. You then create revenue streams that put you in direct contact with your revenue sources.

**Direct Subscription**

This is a straight-forward direct subscription model. Your customers sign up and pay you directly, ideally on a recurring basis. There are many successful newsletters operating this way, as are numerous websites. PeakProsperity.com is a good example of a website that uses a direct subscription model to facilitate access to premium content.

Under this model you are not reliant upon monetizing your content via some third-party platform or system, one that can pull the plug on you at any moment or for any reason.

Because your relationship is directly with your own subscribers, all of them, or a significant portion of them would have to act in concert in order to demonetize you. The odds of this happening are lower given that in order to become your subscriber in the first place they already find your material valuable or otherwise meaningful to themselves.

It may take longer for you to build up your following in this way, however that is a recurring theme of this methodology. We are trading short term gains for longer term resiliency and staying power.

Be aware that the pressure points we discuss elsewhere in this book still apply to you under this model. If you are delivering your content via email, be aware of the choke points within the mailer ecosystem as outlined in **Chapter 10: Your Email.**

The same applies to your payment providers for how you are collecting your subscription revenues.


## SPONSORSHIPS

This is a common model with podcasts and newsletters where you simply solicit corporate sponsors who are aligned with your message and audience. easyDNS sponsored Let's Talk Bitcoin[1] on and off since close to the beginning in 2013 because it fit with our move to be the first ICANN accredited registrar to accept Bitcoin as a payment method.

Again, if somebody wants to attack your revenue model over your message, they have to insert themselves directly between your sponsor and you. This, is in practical terms, usually harder than a group of busybodies simply going to some large, impersonal ad network and getting their unhinged and hysterical version of reality in front of them in order to bully them into making a snap decision.

You usually have some sort of personal contact and relationship with your sponsors. The odds are higher that they will at least pick up the phone or send an email and ask you if there's any substance to what they're being told about you.

## PRODUCTS AND SERVICES

Herein lies one of my secrets to success, one that could easily be an entire book unto itself. In fact, many other books have been written on this exact topic. Joe Pulizzi's Epic Content Marketing and the follow up Content, Inc. come to mind (we have no affiliation with Mr. Pulizzi).

Under this type of model, your content isn't monetized directly, it's all marketing for some other product or service you sell.

Your content drives engagement with your customers, which boosts retention. It enables you to stand out from the crowd, especially if your market segment is crowded or commodified.

Whatever happens in the reaction to your content, *good or bad*, it all serves to cultivate "top of mind awareness" of your brand in the public's mind.

If a backlash ensues against a piece of content you produce in this scenario, the worst outcome isn't deplatforming as much as a boycott. The mobilization is against your customers to incite them to take their business elsewhere.

We discussed boycotts and negative publicity back in **Chapter 4: Does Deplatforming Even Work?**

Content marketing is a tried and true model, with a comparatively wide moat against deplatforming initiatives.

AFFILIATE MARKETING & ENDORSEMENTS

This one is a pretty good way to supplement your revenue streams, but you would need a huge audience to make it your primary source of income. Yet it does happen and it can be done. The entire "mommy blogger" phenomenon was rife with examples of women turning their experiences around motherhood, career, and home life while somehow balancing it all into a full time income. They do it chiefly via affiliate marketing, endorsements and product placements. That's one example, and I'm happy to report that there aren't any ideological adversaries to mommy bloggers that would seek to deplatform them, at least not yet.

Tom Woods [2] is another personality who is a master at this. The libertarian podcaster does a variety of product endorsements which are usually structured as a plug on his podcast along with a coupon code to get a discount on the product. Tom takes things a step further by releasing a number of free courses[3] where he teaches his readers how to do many of the same things he does in terms of monetizing his content.

Here's what I like about affiliate programs and endorsements: the dynamic is somewhat reversed. When somebody goes to the company whose product or service is being promoted by somebody under a deplatform attack, those businesses will know exactly how much money it will cost them to comply with those demands.

Assuming it's a decently performing promoter, companies will be less inclined to play ball when they can see exactly how much the virtue signal will cost them in terms of actual revenues. It may even cost them more than whatever the promoter brings in as they may alienate their base by knuckling under to social justice warriors.

---

You don't have to, and shouldn't, rely on a single method or a single source of revenue as outlined in this section. A good combination of multiple methods and sources will give you the resiliency to survive most setbacks.

After making the mental shift from relying on, and inadvertently promoting other people's platforms, we've consolidated to using domain names and web addresses belonging to you and that you control as your online centre of gravity.

Now there's a new problem. It's the matter of the Single-Point-of-Failure (SPOF). In fact, counselling people to move to this domain based centre-of-gravity model on the surface may run contrary to what DNS providers, such as my company easyDNS, pathologically avoid.

But at some point we have to stick a flag in the ground and understand that our online identity and brand originates from *here,* and then we have to see to it that we can defend that point through anything that may get thrown against it.

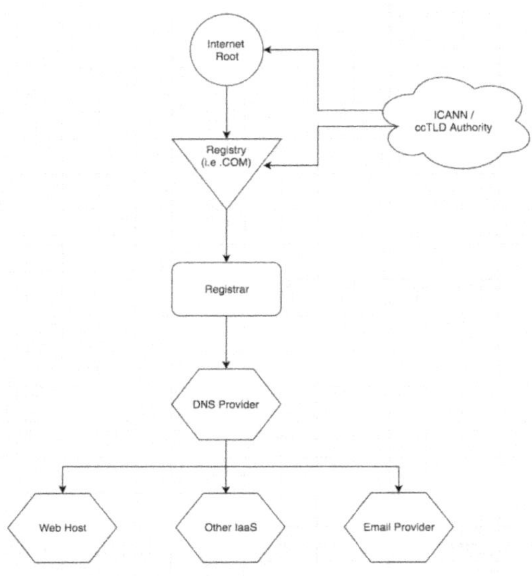


Figure14.1: An Overview of the Domain Name Space

Critics may point out that the Top Level Domain (TLD) portion of a domain, everything to the right of the last dot, such as **.com**, or **.website**, or **.wtf**, denotes a registry, and thus, technically "somebody else's brand". One could then argue that **razorfyre.com** promotes the .com registry, operated by Verisign in a similar fashion to how @razorfyre promotes Twitter.

Point taken. The reality is that everything is interconnected and we can't be completely self-contained islands while simultaneously being visible to the wider world in order to get our message and our content out there.

Among all the alternatives, the DNS system where your domains live is the closest thing that exists in practical terms that:

- is ubiquitous in visibility across the internet and the globe
- is accessible to everybody
- is not dominated by a single entity

While there is a nominal oversight body in ICANN, they do not exert top-down control and they don't monitor or curate content *at all.* At least not yet. The DNS and domain system is the closest thing we have today that resembles a decentralized federation that everybody can access and all technology stacks interoperate with.

---

It is true that this may not be the case forever. There are numerous blockchain based projects that endeavour to create truly decentralized naming structures, such as the early Namecoin project and the Ethereum Name Service (ENS) of today. There is hyperledger and self-sovereign identity (SSI), which look promising and may reach critical mass in the near future.

But at the moment, DNS and owning your own domain names and building out your infrastructure upon them is it. That's where your online center-of-gravity lives, and that's how you own your own racecourse, at least for now.

## THINGS YOU MUST KNOW ABOUT YOUR OWN DOMAINS

What follows is your checklist that you *must* know and information you need to have online for every single domain you operate off of.

*Important Note on Whois Privacy:*
   *If you are using whois privacy (a.k.a domain privacy or any*

*number of other similar terms), be sure that you read and understand the forthcoming section on whois privacy below. If you are using domain privacy because you are under attack because of your content or your views, it is absolutely crucial that you understand the ramifications of utilizing this mechanism.*

## YOUR REGISTRAR

*This is the single-most important decision you'll make regarding where to put your domain names.*

If your web host takes you down, you can switch your DNS at your DNS provider to setup someplace else.

If your DNS provider takes you down, you can switch nameservers, but you have to do that at your registrar.

If your *registrar* takes you down, then you have to move to another registrar, and that's not easy when your domain names are offline completely. You have to be prepared for it in advance, and depending on how badly you are locked into your current registrar, you may need to be working with *another* registrar who will help you get it done.

## LEGAL REGISTRANT

The legal registrant of all your domain names should be *you* or *your organization*, or other legal entity that you control, and that you possess the documentation to prove said control.

Too often, instead of being you, it is one of the following:

- Consultant
- An Employee
- A web host provider

- Any other person who registered the domain that
  isn't you

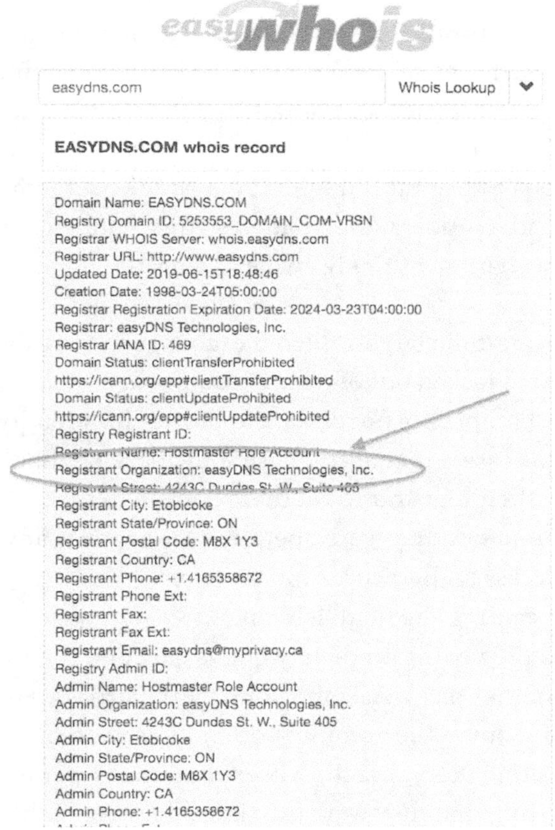


```
easydns.com                          Whois Lookup   ⌄

EASYDNS.COM whois record

Domain Name: EASYDNS.COM
Registry Domain ID: 5253553_DOMAIN_COM-VRSN
Registrar WHOIS Server: whois.easydns.com
Registrar URL: http://www.easydns.com
Updated Date: 2019-06-15T18:48:46
Creation Date: 1998-03-24T05:00:00
Registrar Registration Expiration Date: 2024-03-23T04:00:00
Registrar: easyDNS Technologies, Inc.
Registrar IANA ID: 469
Domain Status: clientTransferProhibited
https://icann.org/epp#clientTransferProhibited
Domain Status: clientUpdateProhibited
https://icann.org/epp#clientUpdateProhibited
Registry Registrant ID:
Registrant Name: Hostmaster Role Account
Registrant Organization: easyDNS Technologies, Inc.
Registrant Street: 4243C Dundas St. W., Suite 405
Registrant City: Etobicoke
Registrant State/Province: ON
Registrant Postal Code: M8X 1Y3
Registrant Country: CA
Registrant Phone: +1.4165358672
Registrant Phone Ext:
Registrant Fax:
Registrant Fax Ext:
Registrant Email: easydns@myprivacy.ca
Registry Admin ID:
Admin Name: Hostmaster Role Account
Admin Organization: easyDNS Technologies, Inc.
Admin Street: 4243C Dundas St. W., Suite 405
Admin City: Etobicoke
Admin State/Province: ON
Admin Postal Code: M8X 1Y3
Admin Country: CA
Admin Phone: +1.4165358672
```

Figure 14.2: Whois record output via https://easywhois.com

Whoever or whatever legal entity listed as the domain registrant is the entity to whom the rights over that domain ultimately accrue.

. . .

**Never provide bogus contact data in a domain registration**

This gets tricky if you're trying to protect your identity for privacy reasons. One thing you should *never* do is put bogus, non-existent contact data in your domain registration details in order to protect your identity associated with your domain names.

If there is a dispute, or you somehow get locked out of your accounts, you have no legal way to prove your identity and regain access to your account or possession over your domains.

Examples of disaster arising directly from this practice are too numerous to list, but I'll mention a couple of them here to help the reader understand that, yes, this happens, and the worst case scenarios routinely ensue as a result:

- The one-time largest Bitcoin exchange in Canada[1] became locked out of their account when their CEO used completely bogus data to protect his identity. In this case, I managed to use some back channels with their registrar to get them back in to their account, but they were operating for over a year with no access to their core domain name.

- One gaming site held held on our system was registered with completely bogus data and then sold to another party. At some point, both parties were locked out of the account, both parties were disputing the transaction itself, both sides were asserting that they were the rightful owner of the domain, and neither had access to the account. Neither party had provided valid contact data. Since nobody could prove they were the entity listed on the account, neither party ever regained access. The domain expired and was promptly re-registered by a domain sniper. Worst possible scenario.

The proper way to shield your name and your contact data from prying eyes, while remaining in compliance with your registrar's Terms of Service *and* ICANN's rules, is to contract with a registrar to use Whois Privacy.

## WHOIS PRIVACY

There are various terms for this, and they all describe a type of de facto unlisted domain. Instead of your identity and contact details being listed, they are replaced by a privacy entity, usually a shell corporation formed by your registrar and listed in its place.

There are various problems with doing this, which we will step through now.

**Ownership:**

Remember what we said earlier: you always want your domains to be registered under your name or your organization and not somebody else. When you enable whois privacy at your registrar, you are doing just that, putting some other entity down as the registrant of your domain.

From my previous book[2], I listed the following table of whois privacy entities based on domain registrar. This is just a small sample. There are over a thousand registrars throughout the world:

| Privacy Entity | Registrar |
| --- | --- |
| Domains By Proxy | Godaddy |
| WhoisGuard | Namecheap |
| MyPrivacy.net Ltd. | easyDNS |
| Contacy Privacy Ltd. | Tucows/OpenSRS |
| WhoisGuard Inc | eNom |
| Oneandone Private Registration | 1&1 Internet Inc |
| Whois Privacy Services Pty Ltd | Fabulous Pty. |
| Protection Service INC d/b/a PrivacyProtect.org | Public Domain Registry |

Source: **Managing Mission Critical Domains & DNS**, Mark Jeftovic / Packt Publishing, 2018.

If you enable whois privacy at your registrar, the registrant for your domain becomes these privacy entities. Your claim to the domain is then abstracted one layer away to the contract between you and your registrar. If it's your registrar who is moving to deplatform you, then you are at a distinct disadvantage.

The reason this is so important is because the registrant is legal controller of the domain (whether as an owner of the domain, in jurisdictions that view domains as property, or as the rights holder in places where domain registration is viewed as a type of leasehold right, like .ca in Canada for example).

**Lock-in:**

Many registrars make it a lot easier to enable whois privacy than to turn it off. They may even make it the default when you register a new domain, or offer it as a "free" add-on. You should check the fine print. Usually it means something like free for the first month, then billed from the second month onward. Or it's offered at some low teaser rate but resets much higher when your domain renews.

However, that's not your main problem. The bigger issue is that in order to transfer your domain away to another registrar, you usually have to disable whois privacy in order to do so.

*IMPORTANT:* Here's the catch. There is a section below called Events that lock your domain, where we will cover the various events that occur over different points in your domain's life cycles which cause your domain to be locked in place for a period of 60 days.

One of those events is when you change the name of the legal registrant of the domain name.

When you disable whois privacy, perhaps in anticipation of moving it out to a new registrar, it is a type of registrant change, and thus, can lock your domain in place for 60 days. That can put the breaks on a transfer, and thwart your objectives if you were trying to stay ahead of a deplatforming attack that may be pressuring your current registrar to take you out.

## Should you use whois privacy?

In my previous book, Managing Mission Critical Domains & DNS[3] (Packt 2018), in the Chapter about whois there are two sub-sections: *Why you should _always_ use whois privacy*, followed by *Why you should _never_ use whois privacy*.

Under certain circumstances, you would be better off turning it on. Under different circumstances, it's better to have it off. Within the context of mitigating against deplatforming attacks, I would decide on whether I'm OK with my identity being known to the world, but I just don't want to be deplatformed versus whether I would rather it not be known who I am at all.

If you're ok with the world knowing who you are, then make sure whois privacy is off, and then populate the registrant contact information with a PO Box that you rent. For the phone number, you can get a VOIP number that goes straight to voice-mail for about $1/month (places like voip.ms), and use an email address under a domain you control, even if it's a special domain you use only for places where you have to provide a valid email contact address (a.k.a a canary email[4].)

You may want to look at incorporating a company and using that as your registrant. It doesn't make you anonymous, but it does put up an additional layer between you and the barbarian hordes.

**Disclosure:**

If you're trying to remain fully anonymous, then use whois privacy. But be aware of the circumstances under which your registrar will:

a) publicly drop the whois privacy on your domain, exposing whatever underlying contact details you have provided, or

b) leave the whois private but furnish the underlying details to third-parties who are requesting it, such as Law Enforcement Agencies (LEA). Do they require a warrant, subpoena or court order, and if so again, does that legal document have to be within the registrar's jurisdiction? Or will they act on a court order from Swaziland?

In the case of easyDNS, we would require any legal order to be served on us in the Province of Ontario. We've seen *fake* court documents from other countries, we've had takedown requests sent from purported police officers in South America emailing us from their cell phones. We've had court orders sent from Russia, in Russian and to this day we still have no idea what they wanted us to do. We've even had the US FDA send us a spreadsheet containing a list of domains to take down that included several Canadian owned domains that were operating under Health Canada approvals.

In other words, we've seen pretty near everything. The only rational way to handle this is to require that all international legal instruments be duly served to us in our home jurisdiction. There are methods for doing that, and when an Ontario Marshall shows up at our door with fully approved Letters Rogatory from another country or US state, we know exactly what has to happen, we know it's legal, and most importantly, we don't have a choice.

Not all registrars operate this way, and if you are going to rely on whois privacy to cloak your identity, you need to know under which circumstances your registrar will drop yours.

## DOMAIN LOCK STATUS

All generic Top Level Domains (gTLDs), like .com, .net, .org and the new ones, .website, .rocks, .wtf and the rest, basically anything that isn't a two-letter country code, have what are called "transfer locks".

When the transfer lock is enabled, any request by another registrar to transfer the domain away will fail, automatically and immediately. This is a good thing, and under most normal circumstances you want this lock to be enabled.

Unfortunately, owing to the rather convoluted possibilities

for various domain states, there isn't a straight forward field in the current whois output that tells you if the domain is locked.

In the whois record depicted below these two fields

```
Domain      Status:      clientTransferProhibited
https://icann.org/epp#clientTransferPro-
hibited
```

```
Domain      Status:        clientUpdateProhibited
https://icann.org/epp#clientUpdateProhibited
```

mean that the domain's transfer lock is indeed on. Counter-intuitively, it *is* rather straightforward to find out if a domain's transfer lock is *off* because:

```
Domain Status: ok https://icann.org/epp#ok
```

It actually *isn't* OK, when the Domain Status displays "ok", unless you really are intending to transfer this domain immi-nently, and you could read this as "it's OK to initiate a transfer".

There are other statuses to watch for. For example, if your domain has suddenly stopped working over the internet, and you look at your whois record and you see this:

```
Domain      Status:    clientHold    https://icann.
org/epp#clientHold
```

· · ·

it means your domain has been suspended by your registrar. It no longer resolves across the internet and nobody can reach your website or send you email. We'll cover what you do if this happens in the **Transferring your domain** section.

## THE AUTH CODE

Every domain under the gTLDs has an associated authentication code. Some ccTLDs also use these, but not all. In order to transfer a domain from one registrar to another you must:

1. unlock the domain's transfer lock
2. provide the authentication code

After that happens, the domain transfer process proceeds as discussed in the **Transferring your domain** section below.

Normally you don't usually see the authentication code in your registrar control panel. There should be way in the dashboard to obtain it. All registrars are obligated under the terms of their Registrar Accreditation Agreement (RAA) to provide this code to you upon request.

Usually this happens by emailing said code to the Administrative Contact email address as listed in the domain's whois record. This is another reason why you want your domain registration's contact email addresses to be valid and under a domain name you control.

The good registrars do this right away (we do). You press the button, you get the code. But be aware that there are other registrars that take liberties here, and can take as long as 72 hours to send you your auth code once you request it. If your domain is with one of these registrars and circumstances suddenly dictate that you need to get out of there fast, this practice can be problematic.

The antidote to this, no matter who you use, is to have a copy of all of your domains auth codes outside of your domain registrar's system. You should also refresh your local copy of your list once a year, in case your registrar has updated the code in the interim.

## YOUR DNS PROVIDER

While your registrar is the entity through whom you obtain a domain name under a given TLD, and then manage its attributes, there's another component to domain names that is required before you can actually use them on the internet.

There's a secret sauce that makes domains an hostnames visible online, and it's called "DNS" (for Domain Name Service). You probably know that websites and email servers have Internet Protocol addresses (IP addresses). DNS is the mechanism that translates human memorable labels, like www.razorfyre.com, to their corresponding IP addresses:

```
MarkLaptop:~ markjeftovic1$ nslookup razorfyre.com
Server:         64.68.203.53
Address:        64.68.203.53#53

Non-authoritative answer:
Name:   razorfyre.com
Address: 64.68.200.44
```

Figure 14.3 A DNS lookup from a UNIX shell

In figure 14.3, I just opened a Unix shell on my laptop and did a quick lookup of our fabled razorfyre.com, and we see that its IP address is 64.68.200.44. Typically, we don't really care what the

IP address is. But internet hosts, routers and gateways all do. In fact, that's *all* they care about when they're shuffling data packets around the internet. The hostname or web address of any given packet isn't looked at until the packet gets all the way to the web hosting server (or email server), and the software there decides what to do with it.

But in order for the internet to function in the way that we've all become accustomed to, in fact dependent on, there needs to be a layer of technology magic that very quickly (typically under 100ms) translates the domain names, website addresses and email addresses from human readable labels we can remember to IP addresses computers and routers understand.

That layer is the DNS, and the specialized machines that do that work are called **nameservers.**

Without this process, nothing would happen online and the internet would not function.

Every domain requires functional DNS to work, but there are multiple parties that typically supply that service for your domains:

- **Domain registrars:** bundle it with your domain registration
- **Web hosts:** often bundle it *and* your domain registration with your web hosting service
- **DNS Providers:** companies that specialize in DNS itself. There's more to it than I've outlined here, but my previous book is an in-depth look at it. It's also what my company easyDNS specializes in.

Given that this all-important function for your domains can be done by a number of different vendors in your setup, it makes it essential that you know exactly who is providing DNS for your domains when it comes time to move away from a hostile vendor or toward a friendly one.

Now that we know the functions of our registrar and how they are different from the functions of our DNS provider, we can look at the permutations of moving your domain from one place to another.


## TRANSFERRING YOUR DOMAIN

We've gone into detail exploring the roles of registrars and DNS providers because these are the two key elements of asserting functional and operational control over your domain names. As has been the core theme of this book, it's these domain names which serve as your overall centre of gravity for your online presence.

Now when it comes time that you want to *move* your domain, it is absolutely crucial that you know how this all works.


### Events that lock your domain

Before we try to move our domains from one place to another, we have to make sure we know what situations will prevent us from doing that. We want to know about them in advance so that we can plan for them. We don't want to find out about them when our hair is on fire.

The following events have the effect of freezing your domain at your current registrar for 60 days:

- The domain is newly registered
- The domain has just completed a registrar transfer
- The listed registrant or admin contact email address has been changed

- The registrar has put the domain on **clientHold** (indefinite)

Transferring your domain in the context here usually means moving it from one registrar (colloquially known as the "losing registrar") to a new one ("gaining registrar"). But it can also mean moving it from one DNS provider to another. In this section we'll show how this dynamic creates three distinct scenarios for moving your domains around and we'll provide step-by-step instructions for how to do it in any scenario.

Under most TLDs, doing a registrar transfer also adds a year onto the expiry date. In other words, a transfer also acts as a renewal or extension.

You do not need to wait for the end of your current registration term to move the domain to another registrar. People who are in mid-term, perhaps with years left on their registration, are sometimes mistakenly hesitant to move to a new registrar because they think they will lose that remaining time with their existing registrar.

It doesn't work like this. The remaining time on your existing term moves with the domain to the new registrar, and then the additional year added on by the transfer extends the term further.

Now, what *might* happen, if your losing registrar is also your **DNS Provider** (see next section), is that they might drop your DNS right away when you transfer away. That can be a problem if you don't handle the transfer correctly, but if you are aware of the various moving parts, you won't get blindsided.

. . .

**Scenario 1):**

- Your losing registrar is also your DNS provider AND
- You want to move both the domain registration and DNS to a new provider who will do both.

Do this:

1. Turn off Whois privacy (if on)
2. (Ask losing registrar to waive any lock to transfer out)
3. (Wait the 60 days if they won't)
4. Unlock your domain (if not already)
5. Get your auth code (transfer code)
6. Set up DNS on new provider
7. Change nameservers on losing registrar to nameservers at gaining registrar
8. Initiate the registrar transfer from gaining registrar side
9. *Make sure you select option to automatically change nameservers to gaining registrar upon transfer*

In this scenario, if your whois privacy was on and your losing registrar insists on locking you in for 60 days after you disable it, you can still, and probably should, switch your DNS to the new provider while you wait it out (Steps 6 and 7). Changing nameservers does not induce any kind of additional lock or freeze period.

**Scenario 2):**

- Your losing registrar is *not* your DNS provider and
- You want to keep your DNS the same after the transfer.

Do this:

1. Turn off Whois privacy (if on)
2. (Ask losing registrar to waive any lock to transfer out)
3. (Wait the 60 days if they won't)
4. Unlock your domain (if not already)
5. Get your auth code (transfer code)
6. Initiate the registrar transfer from gaining registrar side
7. *Make sure you select option to preserve nameservers in transfer (usually this is the default)*

**Scenario 3):**

- You are keeping your registrar the same, but
- you want to move your DNS between providers.

Do this:

1. Setup DNS on new nameservers / DNS provider
2. From your registrar: update your nameservers ("change name server delegation")

TRANSFERRING AWAY FROM A CAPTIVE REGISTRAR

As pointed out at the beginning of this chapter, it's your registrar who exerts the most coercive control over your domains.

Your web host or DNS provider can deplatform you, but they can't stop you from simply moving your content elsewhere (or copying it from your copious backups, which you will maintain after reading the *next* chapter), and setting up elsewhere.

If your registrar takes you down, you are stuck for a while.

Technically, all gTLD and new gTLD registrars *must*, according to their ICANN Registrar Accreditation Agreements (RAAs), allow registrants to move their domains to another registrar.

There are only a narrow set of circumstances under which the captive registrar can refuse to allow you to move your domains. Section 3.1.4(ii) of the ICANN Registrar Transfer Dispute Policy[5] is very clear on these, and they are as follows:

**Fraud.** This specifically means fraud with respect to how the domain was paid for initially with the captive registrar.

If the domain was registered with a stolen credit card or a cheque that bounced, that's fraud and it's a valid reason for the registrar to refuse to allow the domain to transfer away and keep the domain on ice.

What it does *not* mean is that the domain somehow "was engaged in fraudulent activities", and the registrar is keeping it locked on that basis. Doing so invokes the obvious questions of due process, such as "according to whom?" and what legal due process has made a determination that the domain's activities were fraudulent? That line of reasoning was argued in the past, in a case we were involved in[6] (and won), when the resolution panel specifically disallowed it, stating:

---

> The Registrar of Record argued that a basis for withholding the transfer of the domain names was their involvement in fraudulent activity....the reference to "evidence of fraud" in the Transfer Policy does not refer to fraudulent conduct by the holder of the

domain name, but evidence of fraud with respect to the transfer of that domain name. See GNSO Issues Report, Inter-Registrar Transfer Policy Part B at 14-15 (May 15, 2009).

---

The other reasons a captive registrar can deny your request to transfer out are:

- A UDRP or URS proceeding is pending. Those are dispute resolution procedures, such as a claim against your domain that it is violating somebody's trademark. The registrar is obligated in that case to freeze the domain until the case has been decided.
- A pending dispute under the Transfer Dispute Resolution Policy (which is what we're about to talk about below).
- *A court order in a competent jurisdiction* (emphasis added).
- The registrant or administrative contact info is invalid or in dispute. Again, this reinforces why you never use bogus data in your domain registrations.
- Payment dispute
- Express written objection from the domain's owner (either registrant or administrative contact)
- The domain lock is on (along with proof that the registrant has the ability, if desired, to disable the transfer lock)
- The domain is in its 60-day holding period following a change of registrant (discussed earlier).
- Domain is within 60 days of being newly registered.
- Domain has been subject of a prior transfer within 60 days.

Those are the *only* reasons a registrar can refuse to allow you to move your domains away.

Notice that "Antifa says you're a racist" isn't on that list. Granted, a registrar *can,* if they want, take you down for that reason. But they cannot, according to their RAA, stop you from moving away if they do.

But there's a problem. The problem is that the mechanism to dispute a denied transfer request is the **Transfer Dispute Resolution Protocol (TDRP)**[7] and the TDRP can only be invoked by another registrar.

It gets worse.

If you're in a situation where you want to move, and your registrar is uncooperative, *and* you find a new registrar who wants to help, the only way to do it is to take the dispute to arbitration via an ICANN approved dispute resolution provider[8], of which, at the time of writing there are only two: The National Arbitration Forum and the Asian Domain Name Dispute Resolution Centre.

In order to bring a dispute to arbitration, the complainant has to pay the arbitrator first, which can run between $2,000 to $5,000 USD. The loser pays, so if you prevail in your motion, the captive registrar will then have to remit the arbitration fee to the provider, who will then refund the complainant's initial payment.

This flow is new. Back when we did this entire process to free up some names trapped pursuant to a warrantless, emailed request by the City of London Intellectual Property Crime Unit there was an intermediary step. Before going to arbitration, the new registrar could make a Request For Enforcement (RFE) to the registry directly. When we did it, the registry deferred decision (literally issuing a decision of "no decision") and we had to pony up and take it to arbitration anyway. But at least that first step didn't cost thousands of dollars and, on occasion simply telling the captive registrar you were filing an RFE was enough to get the domain released.

It's easier to pick a registrar in the first place who won't take your domains down for arbitrary or capricious reasons. If you have any doubts regarding a particular registrar, you can do the following. Simply open a support ticket and ask them what their policy is. Tell them your use case, the kind of content you will be publishing and what their policy is toward it, and inquire what their takedown policy is.

You will know where you stand ahead of onboarding and get the additional benefit of putting their support desk through some paces to get a feel for their responsiveness.

## YOUR REGISTRY OR TOP LEVEL DOMAIN (TLD)

The domain registry is the operator of the Top Level Domain (TLD), everything to the right of the ".".

Examples:

| Domain | TLD | Registry / Operator |
| --- | --- | --- |
| example.com | .COM | Verisign |
| example.ca | .CA | CIRA |
| example.co | .CO | .CO Internet S.A.S (Colombia) |
| example.tv | .TV | Versign (Tuvalu) |
| example.ly | .LY | NIC.ly (Libya) |
| example.wtf | .WTF | Donuts Inc. |

Figure 14.5 Example domains, TLDs and registry operators

If the TLD is two characters, as in some of our examples above, then they are country-code TLDs. Each country that has an ISO3166 postal code[9] has their corresponding two character code assigned to their internet top level domain.

Each country makes their own rules about how their domains are governed, while the rest of the TLDs like .com, .website, .wtf and the rest are governed by rules set by ICANN, a non-profit California corporation that oversees the global naming and IP numbering infrastructure.

Everything we describe above with respect to registrars applies to all TLDs under the provenance of ICANN.

---

Country code domains are balkanized across varying rulesets and governance structures, but if you're going to pick one of these exotic ccTLD's for your online identity (.ly, .io, .tv, .fm, etc) then you need to be aware that you are operating at the pleasure of those countries' governments.

There have been episodes in the past, where suddenly the fate of numerous Silicon Valley startups became uncertain because of this. For example, the URL shortener bit.ly, as well as all of the other ".ly" companies, got a scare when the Arab Spring visited Libya.[10] As the government desperately tried to get control of the narrative by shutting down large portions of the domestic internet, there was speculation that in a worst case scenario, the .ly TLD could go offline completely.

It didn't happen, but there had been a precedent that warranted concern. The Libyan government *did* summarily terminate another URL shortener, **vb.ly**[11], citing Sharia law and that the service was being used for redirecting pornographic URLs.

In other words, a San Francisco based URL shortener got deplatformed by an African government citing Sharia law, all because of their choice of top level domain.

More recently the UN condemned the UK's occupation of the Chagos Islands (a part of the British Indian Ocean Territory).

What would happen to its **.io** TLD if Britain were to eventually relinquish that territory and the country code changes?[12] The **.io** TLD is a favourite among tech startups and if it were to be rescinded, it would cause significant disruption.

While I personally consider this outcome to be low probability (note that even though the Soviet Union's TLD changed from **.su** to the Russian Federation's **.ru**, the .su TLD still remains grandfatherered into the internet root), Pascal's Wager applies: though the probability is remote, the consequences are significant.

---

If your goal is to be unassailable, then register your key domains under an ICANN sponsored TLD so you can at least get a handle on the rules you are going to be operating under.

It would be remiss of me to counsel the reader to take control over their online identity, to set up their center-of-gravity on a domain name they own and control, to have all your videos, articles, ebooks, podcasts and any other material all available from your central website, and then not talk about backing up all of that in case something happens to your website or your main domain.

The model is very simple. It can guarantee that you prevent irrecoverable disasters, and yet, few people, even relatively few businesses and organizations, actually do it:

1. Backup your central websites, data, source code and configuration files
2. Backup your laptops, desktops and any other devices where you create your content
3. Backup your backups

You can usually backup your websites and your blogs with your hosting provider and also via third-party services. Another reason why I generally recommend Wordpress for managing your content is because there are numerous plugins to backup your Wordpress sites, all the way from VaultPress (which is now owned by Wordpress's parent company and part of the JetPack suite), to Blogvault and even the native "Export" function within Wordpress lets you manually grab a copy of your posts, pages, themes and data.

Personally, I 'm biased toward Blogvault. When I built out my wife's website for her debut novel[1], I figured I better have it backed up, because if anything happened to it and I didn't have a backup, I'd be on the couch for life.

I liked it so much I ended up doing a deal with them to bundle Blogvault with our own easyPress (hosted Wordpress) packages. So all of our customers' sites have complete synced backups, plugin management, staging sites and Web Application Firewall. The works.

If you are running your own servers, perhaps as outlined in an earlier section, then it goes without saying you need to be backing those up as well.

Some server level backup solutions include:

- Acronis
- Capterra
- Carbonite
- OpenDrive

I prefer at least two separate backup solutions for the servers. You can use a comparatively inexpensive data archive solution for the second backup. These services are not intended for rapid restore from the cloud, but rather, to have access to rarely accessed data (similar to old fashioned tape backups) and prior revisions of your entire enterprise in the event of absolute, total catastrophic failure.

Most of the data archive services are from the major enterprise providers like Amazon's Glacier, Oracle and Microsoft Azure.

Finally, you need to backup your work stations, laptops or any other device you use personally to create your content. I use a combination of cloud based backups (such as Backblaze), native Apple time machine backups in the house, and for safety I have some commodity external drives that connect to my laptop when I dock at home or my office which sync my data and files continually.

In addition to defending ourselves on the incumbent platforms, Facebook, Twitter, et al, we should also look at gaining a foothold in as many rising challenger platforms as practical. Granted, none of these have near the reach of the incumbents, and most never will.

But it helps to have that presence on alternative platforms because if you do experience a setback on the mainstream ones, people will increasingly turn to the alternatives to find you. This is especially true if your deplatforming has been high profile and the Streisand Effect is kicking in.

---

## MASTODON

Mastodon is a decentralized alternative to Twitter that is arranged as a federation. "The fediverse" as the users call it. Anybody can run a node, it's open source, it's free, or you can just join somebody else's node by creating an account there.

Each node sets its own community standards, so you can probably find one that suits your proclivities and style. Individual nodes can control who they peer with so everybody can make decisions *for themselves* around what is or isn't desirable content.

What you can also do is use a tool like Moa.party to link your Twitter account with your Mastodon id. Then whatever you tweet on one system, goes out via the other as well. This can be useful in case your Twitter account gets suspended there would still be a record of all your tweets on your Mastodon feed.

I was pleasantly surprised to notice recently that somewhere along the line my follower count on Mastodon is suddenly more than double what it is on Twitter.

*(easyDNS is a Mastodon gold sponsor and runs a node where you can set up a free account at https://nojack.easydns.ca )*

## GAB

Gab may be the largest Twitter challenger in existence at the time of writing. But the network has been fraught with deplatforming challenges itself. Frequently touted in the mainstream media as a haven for the alt-right, Gab has found itself losing its domain names, its network hosting and having their apps removed from the iTunes store.

I attribute Gab's tribulations to some unforced errors which didn't help their own case. However, the seemingly coordinated industry machinations against them are troublesome, and the reality is they continue to bounce back stronger than ever (Streisand Effect, once again).

## TELEGRAM

Initially an encrypted VoIP and messaging platform, Telegram[1] is increasingly being used as a broadcasting platform akin to microblogging using its channels and group collaboration with chats.

Shortly after this book was published Zerohedge was suspended from Twitter[2] and set up a group[3] on Telegram.

Telegram claims over 200 million users globally.

We're in the process of setting up an experimental Telegram group for our AxisOfEasy channel: https://t.me/AxisOfEasy


## KEYBASE

Similar to Telegram, Keybase[4] is an encrypted communications application. It is open source (Telegram's clients are open source but the central server is not). Keybase is encrypted and allows you to create secure channels, file servers and group chats.


## STEEMIT

Steemit was co-founded by crypto-currency pioneer Dan Larimer. It was possibly the first platform that attempted to enable content creators to directly monetize their material through a native micropayments system. The system uses its own blockchain which underpins the crypto-currency STEEM. At the time of writing, Steemit has in excess of 1.2 million registered users.

The WYSIWYG editor for creating posts seems similar to Medium's (which I do not recommend, btw, as they are known to arbitrarily deplatform content creators) and supports various markdown notations, but it's not as frictionless.

Overall, it's a work in progress, but in my mind on the right track. There is a decent amount of activity and signal here.

## MINDS

Minds.com is more like a Facebook type platform, with its own token system that is used to run the advertising network. The token is called Minds and is an Ethereum ERC-20 token. The ad network is called Boost. Content creators can earn Minds tokens directly for their content as it is shared through the network.

What's interesting about Minds is the content moderation policy[5], which includes an appeals process in which twelve peers from the userbase itself have the ability to overturn previous decisions.

## MEWE

Billing itself as "The Next-Gen Social Network", MeWe pledges to be free to join in perpetuity and to never monetize its users' privacy. The groups available and the membership and content looks more diverse and general. The dashboard is slick, akin to a Facebook moreso than a Twitter. I forgot I had an account on MeWe until I started compiling this list, so now I'm exploring it again.

## PEEP.ETH

Peepeth[6] is a microblogging system that is based on the Ethererum blockchain. In order to use it you need to have visibility to the Ethereum blockchain, such as accessing it via an dapp browser[7] or with a browser plugin like Metamask[8].

Most of the signal here is steeped in Ethereum and the associated subculture.

FLOTE.APP

Looks like a Twitter alternative, low volume at the moment and fairly saturated with libertarians, anarcho-capitalists and crypto punks .The signal-to-noise ratio looks very healthy from that perspective and, by contrast, it seems to be almost devoid of that alt-right timbre that permeates Gab.

As a libertarian, I've wrestled with this issue for a long time. Companies are free to do what they want with their property, aren't they?

Staunch statists will be the first to tell you, "free speech" isn't about being able to say whatever you want on social media. The guarantees of free speech are to protect citizens from *their governments*, not from Facebook.

It's a complicated issue, one that even libertarians disagree on.

As I sat down at the end of the writing journey for this book, which ended up clocking in around 200 pages instead of the 15 or 20 I originally planned, I realized it really doesn't matter.

The only thing that matters is what the current situation is, and what we as content creators, dissidents and contrarians can do to mitigate against current conditions.

My belief is firm that over time, these seemingly invincible tech giants are, through their capriciousness and unreliability, incentivizing their own disruption. So it's to be expected and understandable that the incumbents cling fervently to whatever levers they can to remain in control. They know viscerally how fast old orders are swept away in this environment.

I have no real idea what comes next. Nobody does. And that is precisely why it is important for every content producer, for every dissident voice, to remain active and to put those alternative narratives out there, so that those who are willing to look outside the cone of approved media can discover them and see the wider possibilities.


WHAT TO DO NEXT

If you have a burning desire to be a part of the vanguard, to connect with like-minded content creators and to be part of a wider community, head on over to AxisOfEasy.com and first, sign up for the weekly digest newsletter.

We are currently building out a standalone site for AxisOfEasy, separate from our corporate mothership at easyDNS.com, and we will be creating a community forum there to track and discuss our progress in these seemingly never-ending culture wars.

Mark Jeftovic is the co-founder and CEO of easyDNS Technologies Inc, an ICANN accredited domain registrar and managed DNS provider based in Toronto, Canada. Founded in 1998, the company also provides web and email hosting, along with a recently launched domain security and monitoring dashboard called *Domainsure.*

The easyDNS mantra since the very beginning has been: **We kill lock-in in all its forms.**

Jeftovic has served as director to the Canadian Internet Registration Authority (CIRA), the body that oversees the .CA top level domain, and is currently a director with the Internet Society, Canada Chapter.

An early Bitcoin and crypto-currency enthusiast, easyDNS was the first ICANN registrar to accept Bitcoin, and the first to support Ethereum Name Service (ENS) enabled domains. Jeftovic participates in the Ethereum Name Service Working Group.

He is the author of **Managing Mission Critical Domains & DNS** via Packt Publishing (2018) and blogs about the convergence of economics, technology and history via GuerrillaCapitalism.com.

Jeftovic ran as a candidate for the Libertarian Party of Canada in the 2015 Federal Election in the Parkdale/High-Park riding.

Mark is married to the novelist Angela Applewhite and they live in Toronto with their daughter, Emily.

CONTACT:


Email: mark@jeftovic.net
Mastodon: https://nojack.easydns.ca/@stuntpope
Twitter: @stuntpope

APPENDIX A: SELECTED WRITINGS_

What follows are some selected writings over the years from the easyDNS blog, and elsewhere, that speak to some of the issues around deplatforming, cancel culture and free speech.

Where appropriate I have added some commentary or minor edits.

# FIRST THEY CAME FOR THE FILE SHARING DOMAINS_

COMMENTARY

*An obvious riff on the Martin Niemöller poem "First They Came For the Socialists".*[1]

*What I got wrong here was that I assumed at the time that the Big Tech platforms would also come under the ire of Big Brother. What has happened instead is that they became either complicit, or co-opted within the mechanisms of increasing surveillance and societal control. Google, Facebook, Twitter and even Wikipedia are more part of the apparatus now, as opposed to being liberators.*

---

FIRST THEY CAME FOR THE FILE-SHARING DOMAINS...

*November 27, 2010*

*(Via https://easydns.com/blog/2010/11/27/first-they-came-for-the-file-sharing-domains/ )*

First, they came for the file-sharing websites, because they were infringing on copyright. (I didn't care, because I didn't share files).

Then, they came for the illegal offshore pharmacies, because they were facilitating the import of dangerous generic pharmaceuticals that massively undercut the name brand companies. (I didn't care because I didn't buy generic drugs)

These first choices may have seemed odd, because there were far worse things out there on the internet to go after. However, since nobody cared too much about the file-sharing sites and the illegal generic pharmacies, they figured it was safe to take things up a notch....

So even worse things were gone after.....

Next, they came for the terrorist websites. And since criticizing the government was itself considered an act of terrorism, it meant the end for everything ranging from WikiLeaks to LewRockell.com (I didn't mind, because I didn't follow those websites).

By now, the economic malaise that began in the first decade of the new century was well into its second decade and the culprit for this was clearly known to be financial speculators, short sellers and contrarians.

So then they came for the websites that disseminated unofficial economic data. Bye bye ShadowStats, Zerohedge and a whole host of others. (But I didn't care, because I was still sore from losing all my money in the housing bubble crash)

But "illegal dissent" was still rife on the internet (perhaps even more so, for some reason....)

Because constitutionalists, legal scholars and other dangerous cranks were sowing dissent and challenging the actions of Homeland Security, they came for the websites that facilitated "criminal online assembly", "unlawful collusion" and "non-sanctioned collaboration". That was the end of Facebook, Twitter and a host of others. (Not that I minded, I was never much into all those "social" websites...)

Then they needed to  do something about websites that provided "tools to access criminal content".

That's when they came for Google. (That was OK, I had all the stuff I accessed bookmarked anyway)

Then they came for my neighbour's website, because they said his blog was pernicious and unauthorized. (He was kind of weird, so it didn't really bother me).

Finally, they came for me. (And nobody else cared.)

Because nothing had stopped them before and they could do whatever they want.

# THE CULTURAL PURGE WILL NOT BE TELEVISED_

COMMENTARY

*This was written when I was first detecting that their was a cultural purge underway. It was surprising to me, I expected as much to occur after the 2016 US election. However, I, like everybody else, was not expecting that outcome. So what was surprising to me was that the election going "the wrong way" didn't head off the cultural purge I was dreading; instead it ignited it.*

*As a case-in-point, this article, when posted to HackerNews[1] it immediately began climbing fast with lots of up votes. Yet it was repeatedly being flagged as inappropriate (a designation intended for completely unacceptable material such as spam or pornography). When it was finally permanently de-flagged by admins, it rocketed straight to the front page of HackerNews.*

THE CULTURAL PURGE WILL NOT BE TELEVISED

*February 24, 2017*

*"The conscious and intelligent manipulation of the organized habits and opinions of the masses is an important element in democratic society. Those who manipulate this unseen mechanism of society constitute an invisible government which is the true ruling power of our country.*

*We are governed, our minds are molded, our tastes formed, and our ideas suggested, largely by men we have never heard of.... It is they who pull the wires that control the public mind."*

— EDWARD BERNAYS, PUBLIC RELATIONS

I've been trying not to write this post, because really, who needs a bunch of shrill, hysterical snowflakes calling you a racist nazi for committing the egregious sin of pointing out the many contradictions in the #deleteshopify boycott and the wider witch hunt mentality that pervades social discourse these days?

The main factor holding me back is not cynicism but actually *fear*. For the first time in my life, I'm afraid to speak my mind. The possible ramifications of exercising my inalienable right to free speech frighten the crap out of me. So much so that I really don't want to do it. I've become known as the type of person who speaks candidly and frankly about some tough issues, and I've never had a problem doing that in the past. I've gone up against some pretty intimidating forces, such as the City of London IPCU and the US FDA, but I've never been as scared as I am now to speak out. For that reason I'm just going to have to suck it up and do it.

**There is a cultural purge in progress.**

It is directed against not only those who are perceived as "pro-

Trump" (which as a card carrying Libertarian I am not - I think that he's no friend to free speech, privacy or the internet), but targeting even those who are not "anti-Trump *enough*".

This cultural purge has a two-pronged approach. From one side, from elements within the corridors of power (or those recently ejected from it) who have successfully floated the concept that free speech is not inviolable and that it would be a good thing for "truth" to be curated by "somebody" who knows better:

---

*"We are going to have to rebuild within this wild-wild-west-of-information flow **some sort of curating function** that people agree to... There has to be, I think, some sort of **way in which we can sort through information that passes some basic truthiness tests and those that we have to discard,** because they just don't have any basis in anything that's actually happening in the world...That is hard to do, but **I think it's going to be necessary, it's going to be possible,"***

- BARACK OBAMA IN SPEECH AT FRONTIERS
CONFERENCE, PITTSBURGH, PA, OCT 13, 2016
(EMPHASIS ADDED)

---

The other half comes from the trenches, comprised of manic flashmobs directing enmity against, literally, anything *remotely connected* to those deemed responsible for the greatest political upset of our time.

The mainstream media, outlets like the Washington Post and the New York Times, among others, are complicit, providing the glue or the lubricant between this pincer movement and its chilling effects. The combination gels into an echo chamber drowning out all rationality and renders differing philosophies and legitimate dissent as blasphemous.

Let me explain my choice of title for this post and how it captures what I see going on here:

This post title is obviously a riff on Gil Scott-Heron's song 'The Revolution Will Not Be Televised', and the backstory behind this song is quite instructive to times like these:

Gil Scott-Heron saw first hand how altruistically motivated social activism can turn ugly when a campus protest action he initiated went horribly overboard. After the death of one of Scott-Heron's schoolmates, he started a grass roots movement with the goal of improving the medial conditions on his campus, including making the college infirmary operate 24×7, something he felt would have saved his friend's life.

The laudable aim of improving conditions on campus with the possibility of saving future lives derailed into a menacing fracas. A mob congregated on the front lawn of the infirmary doctor's home where they proceeded to *burn him in effigy*:

---

*"The protest grew angry, culminating with some students hanging the doctor in effigy from a tree in his front yard and setting it on fire. The doctor came out of his house and swore that he wasn't responsible for the deaths. As he proclaimed his innocence, he had tears in his eyes.*

*When Gil arrived at the protest, he stood between the students and the doctor, looking at the doctor's children staring out the window in fear. 'A cold flash scampered across the back of my neck', wrote Gil later to describe his sudden fear that events could spiral out of control into violence, a fear which was allayed only when the students went back to their dorms.*

*The realization that radical action sometimes leads to unintended consequences and violent overreactions haunted*

*Gil, and that image of a distraught Dr. Davies lingered in his mind for months to come. The experience reinforced Gil's instinct to avoid violence and militant action in the struggle for social change."*

- WHY GIL SCOTT-HERON WROTE "THE REVOLUTION<br>WILL NOT BE TELEVISED" BY MARCUS BARAM

---

One should easily concede that today there are many reasons to petition for change. Our governments still have us all under wholesale surveillance, we are still involved in numerous unsanctioned wars, we continue to be provoked toward new ones, and the government continues to methodically destroy the economy via financial repression.

But we should all take Gil Scott-Heron's lesson to heart and try to keep in mind that we are all human beings. We all have rights and we should all be secure in our ability to speak and associate freely.

## BUT THAT ISN'T WHAT'S HAPPENING...

Today, the mainstream media, rather than objectively and rationally report on facts, is instead complicit in a sustained, wide-ranging campaign of demonization of "all things non-Democrat". There is blanket categorical denial of any valid basis for why the citizens worldwide are rejecting what they increasingly see as an "Establishment Elite" agenda.

Greece, Brexit, Trump, and quite possibly soon, Marine Le Pen in France, are all continuations of a theme. These events are referendums unto themselves and those "Global Elites" are on a losing streak. Instead of trying to understand the basis of these rejections (that the populace are sick and tired of having a two-tiered society in which their civil rights are eroded and they get saddled with all the debt, while the elites get to operate under a different set of rules and gobble up all the assets), they have mounted a concerted campaign of outright propaganda and mind-numbingly nonsensical narratives to dismiss away these acts of "defiance".

As alt-market.com's Brandon Smith commentary observes:

---

*"One of the most favored propaganda tactics of establishment elites and [those] they employ ... **is to relabel or redefine an opponent before they can solidly define themselves**. In other words, elites [and their media] will seek to "brand" you (just as corporations use branding) in the minds of the masses so that **they can take away your ability to define yourself as anything else**." (emphasis added)*

---

And this is exactly what's happening. For example, when you say "Breitbart", your average person is so inculcated from the repetition of the words "white supremacist", "racist" and "nazi", that people just assume that's what it is. From there, people think that it's OK to #boycottshopify simply for supplying basic online ecommerce services to them. (Where does it stop? By the way, Breitbart derives 100% of its revenues from the internet. Perhaps everybody in a twist about it should do us all a favour and boycott that too.)

Is Breitbart really a white supremacist, racist nazi hate site? Actually, no it isn't. Many people think it is, however, because they've been conditioned to believe it, and they've never actually gone there to see for themselves.

How do I know that Breitbart isn't really the white supremacist, neo-nazi hate-site that we are incessantly brainwashed  to believe it is? Well for one thing, I've seen the real deal. They look like this:

This place is called "Sh*tskin Plantation". They wound up on easyDNS (my company's system ) for about a week by the time we kicked them. The fact that we did eject a real honest to god racist, neo-nazi hate site doesn't bolster the #boycottshopify movement for three reasons:

1. Sh*tskin Plantation is clearly racist and contains actual language condoning violence toward an identifiable group. It was right there for anybody to see. Here in Canada, such material is codified into law as "hate speech" under the Criminal Code.

2. *We chose.* We assessed our AUP, found them in violation and kicked them. Specifically we found them in violation of "the Non-Aggression Principle" in our Plain English Terms of Service. The NAP has grey areas and subjective rabbit holes. Libertarians debate it relentlessly. But the important thing is that nobody else forced us to do it in the absence of due process. We made our own determination, and that's important. Sacrosanct, in fact.

3. Breitbart is an ultra-conservative, right-wing political opinion site. That's all. They seem to have a penchant for inflammatory, click-bait headlines, but

who doesn't these days? You may not like it, I may not like it, but they absolutely have the right to be online and to publish.

That anybody who has even the most tenuous affiliation with them is fair game for having their rights curtailed, their livelihood sanctioned or sabotaged, is indefensible. The only legitimate mechanism for these people to suffer in their fortunes is through the failure of their ideas in the marketplace of thought. By being *rejected*, not through being *repressed* (see below).

It is entirely reasonable for Shopify, or  any other vendor, to keep supplying services to Breitbart (at present they have no services with easyDNS).

It is *also* reasonable for any of those vendors to choose not to supply services to them of their own volition (you can't have it both ways folks, you can't force Shopify to dump Breitbart and simultaneously force some Bible-thumping redneck to bake a cake for a gay wedding).

What *isn't* reasonable is to coerce or compel anybody else to take any action they would not themselves take under their own judgement. It's truly frightening that there is a growing sentiment that this is acceptable behaviour.

---

*Do you really want to live in a world where people sever business and personal relationships because a literal flash mob demands it? Where mobs get to pick and choose who you are allowed to associate with?*

Shopify has over 300,000 customers. You honestly expect them to sort through those and kick out the ones that *you* think are morally objectionable?

In 2010, when easyDNS was itself embroiled in the Wikileaks debacle, I was absolutely appalled when ranking politicians applauded the vendors for severing ties with them. Senator Lieberman congratulated Amazon and PayPal by name for *"breaking their contracts"*. He literally used those words. Here was a ranking politician applauding behaviour that should rightly get you sued.

The public backlash then was huge and pro-Wikileaks. In our own small way, we stood up for Wikileaks then and we maintain a congruent position now. I applaud Shopify for standing firm and refusing to sever their ties for the same reason.

## THE "RIGHT SIDE" OF HISTORY

Whenever I hear a lot of activists whining about the current situation, I frequently hear references to being "on the right side of history". Nobody wants to be on the wrong side of *that*.

Actually, that's a nonsensical statement since history is amoral, or as Winston Churchill famously observed, *"One damned thing after another"*.

However, there is one rule of thumb I've formulated over the years, which I think can keep one onside of the grand currents sweeping through time and society and helped me understand my sympathy with Libertarianism and anarcho-capitalism. That is to know the fine line between *rejecting* an idea that one finds immoral, unethical, obsolete or otherwise objectionable and *repressing* it.

Morality is largely subjective. Very few people act in a way they themselves consider immoral. Almost everybody thinks that whatever they're doing, they're on the side of the angels. The tiny sliver of participants who are fully cognizant of their own immoral actions and proceed anyway are criminals and sociopaths (the majority of *them* gravitate into politics).

When enough people's ethical compasses align, you get a cultural or societal norm. One of the cultural norms that we fought hard for over the ages was that people have a right to free speech and free association. You can disagree with what I have to say but respect my right to say it.

These rights were so hard won that they were codified into universal laws and into the very constitutions that govern most civilized nations. I believe one of the more well-known words for it is "inalienable".

Until now. Now people are putting conditions around "free speech" and "free association".

The idea that free speech has its limits somewhere around the point where it hurts somebody's feelings is beyond idiotic and dangerous.

**Tweet of person exercising her free speech to encourage economic harm to others...**

The world is not one big foam insulated, bubble wrapped

safe space. This may come as a shock to you, but there is a widespread sentiment, *a backlash* dare I say, against the idea that a Saviour State should watch over everything and smooth out all the world's sharp edges.

Besides...

## BOYCOTTS USUALLY BACKFIRE.

Back in the mid-90s, Bob Rae was the Premiere of Ontario, and I was in a failed metal band out of London, Ontario. Mr. Rae wrote a nice song about multiculturalism called "Same Boat Now" and submitted it to various record labels who promptly rejected it and told him not to quit his day job.

My band recorded a power-pop version of his song and released it on 7" vinyl. Our label  put an open letter to Mr. Rae on the back sleeve that was highly critical of his socialist political platform (albeit quite tame by today's standards).

I was mortified, fearing a media backlash, but felt trapped. I called Jack Richardson, my former college prof from Fanshawe College's Music Industry Arts program and widely credited with having single-handedly created the Canadian music industry, and asked his advice.

Before I finished relaying the details, he was laughing. "Mark", he said, "the only thing that truly matters is that they spell 'Landslide' right. That's it".

This has been borne out countless times since that event. I could list them here, but the point is boycotts usually invoke The Streisand Effect and actually bolster the target of the boycott. We can cite a couple brief examples:

- During the Bob Parsons era of GoDaddy, when he shot the elephant, or when he aired some super-sexist Super Bowl commercial, GoDaddy numbers, in terms of net-new domains-in or registered, usually went up, not down, in the face of consumer outrage and boycotts.

- Wikileaks, again – when we did help their mirror sites get back online, there was a counter-reaction against that. Every once in a while I check the domains from the customers who sent me extremely hostile emails telling me they were leaving, and almost all of them remained (and some still do) customers to this day.

- Shopify itself, who is publicly traded, has been on a tear in share price for most of the year, and it's continued unabated since  #deleteShopify began.

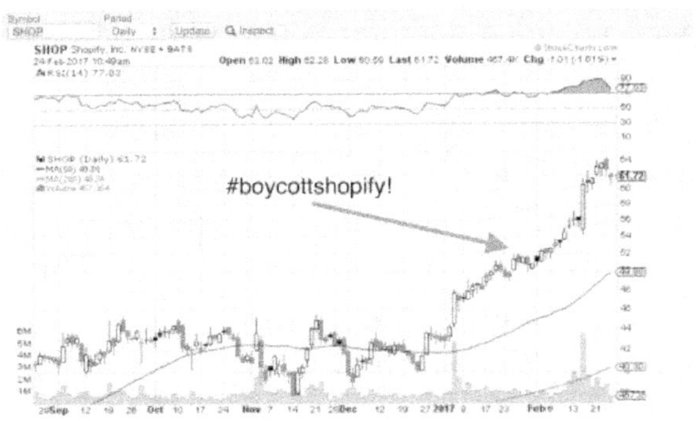


## SO WHAT CAN YOU DO?

You can only govern yourself. Your only recourse is whether to associate or disassociate with somebody. Yes, you are perfectly within your rights to #boycottshopify, but as I've outlined, you're being naive in doing so and you will likely have the exact opposite effect if you're enough of a loudmouth about it .

But if this Cultural Purge proceeds we will actually, for real, lose what used to be inalienable rights. Our right to free speech, our right to free association, and our rights to our own minds. If something you say is considered "hurtful" (which will more closely resemble dissent or criticism of the Official Narrative than anything else), you will be sanctioned. You will tow the line or you will be penalized – contracts severed, vendors disassociate themselves, boycotts ensue. Whatever you do, just don't say or think the wrong thing, because not going along with the crowd will make you a *pariah*.

If you want to prevent this:

- 1) You have the duty to look at the issue first hand and decide for yourself if it has any merit. Don't ever come to me and tell me "XYZ is white supremacist, neo-nazi hate speech", unless you can show me an article that has the hate speech in it. Show me the white supremacist rhetoric. If you tell me you believe it simply because that's what WaPo told you, then you are a fool. You are WaPo's useful idiot. A WaPobot.

- 2) You have to be prepared to call BS whenever some whining snowflake demands safety from any contrary opinion, whenever some pundit robotically repeats the "white supremacist, hate speech, homophobe, Russian hackers" mantra, and whenever you're asked to jump on some witchunt bandwagon against someone who dares to dispute the Official Narrative.

- 3) You have to be able to take the heat. Guess what? You'll be next. Speak out against this nonsense, and you'll be subjected to hysterionics, character assassination, guilt by the most tenuous of associations, distortions of fact and a co-ordinated piling on by mobs of unquestioning ideological berserkers.

- You'll be Peter Thiel: there was a popular outcry to remove him from Facebook's board, why? Because he endorsed Trump.
- You'll be Scott Adams: his crime? Correctly predicting that Trump was going to win.
- You'll be Ivanka Trump: facing a co-ordinated attack on her livelihood for her transgression of being born a Trump.

That is a cultural purge.

Hell, *I'm* probably next just for writing this piece. So be it. My credibility as a non-racist, free-speech Libertarian is unassailable, and I am categorically unaffiliated with Russian intelligence. My duty is to speak out precisely because it is becoming more dangerous to speak out.

---

"In times of universal deceit, telling the truth is a revolutionary act".

– UNKNOWN

---

# A HERETIC'S GUIDE TO DEPLATFORMING_

## COMMENTARY

*As the deplatforming phenomenon intensified, it became more troubling. I wrote **A Heretic's Guide to Deplatforming** in the face of what seemed like a coordinated effort among the Silicon Valley "in-club" to remove the Twitter alternative Gab from the internet.*

*Once again, it went to the front page of HackerNews, but only after those who didn't want to hear what we had to say did their best to prevent that, by flagging the post as "inappropriate" until moderators stepped in to prevent that.*

---

## A HERETIC'S GUIDE TO DEPLATFORMING

The phenomenon of deplatforming in the internet age, which includes the component of publicly expressed outrage that impels companies to act to remove objectionable content, provides ample fodder for getting all kinds of things wrong against the backdrop of people wanting to put things right.

To that end I see three distinct themes around it:

1. We run the risk that the act of deplatforming can become as extreme as the hate speech it seeks to banish.
2. While it's within the purview of every private (and by that I mean non-governmental) company to do it, those who do typically undermine their own long term interests. And,
3. On our present course, we're headed for a balkanized social media landscape

The idea of mobilizing public support, usually just raw emotion, and channeling it toward denying service or infrastructure to something deemed undesirable has taken on an almost macabre element in this day and age. The problem with deplatforming is nobody can give you an objective, rule-of-thumb based guideline that can answer the question

## "WHERE DOES IT STOP?"

In the latest issue of #AxisOfEasy I mentioned the recent deplatforming of Gab and offhandedly asked readers to reply back to me if they had any thoughts around it. The responses I've gotten were all, in-depth, long, thoughtful, considered and rational. I'd like to quote one at length:

---

*"...the lines are getting blurrier and blurrier. When we hold someone socially accountable for something they say, or some idea they espouse — and we do so by way of silencing them or terminating services of any kind to them, a few things happen. First, we may be seen as exercising our own right to freely speak (and sure, why not?). Second, we haven't turned that*

*mind around and instead driving the thing underground (where it can and does continue to fester). Third, we willfully and purposefully exercise an act of control over someone else — an act that in actuality we may or may not have a right to. This third point is the blurriest, and it may simply have no good single answer.*

*The more frightful thing that seems to be happening is that now we not only hold the individual responsible, but the platform itself responsible. Why? Should the ISP that serves the user's connection also be responsible for letting that person even access the Internet? Should the email service provider not share in the blame, by allowing that individual the continued ability to communicate with those he or she forms such thoughts and ideas with? If a group rents equipment to loudly broadcast its ideas, or purchases the paper and supplies necessary for its signs, would we or should we hold the suppliers of these things responsible if the group is deemed toxic? How far down the social-justice rabbit-hole can and should we, the society, go? Where will it end?"*

---

The reality is that an effective deplatforming initiative is built primarily on the momentum of rage and angst, and as it gathers momentum, fewer and fewer participants have the presence of mind to approach the subject at hand rationally and objectively. It is, as Elias Canetti termed it, a type of hunting pack known as "the baiting crowd".

---

*"The baiting crowd forms with reference to a quickly attainable goal. That goal is widely known and clearly marked, and it is also near. This crowd is out for killing and it knows whom it wants to kill. It heads for this goal with unique determination and cannot be cheated of it. The*

*proclaiming of the goal, the spreading about of who it is that is to perish, is enough to make the crowd form. The concentration on killing is of a special kind of unsurpassed intensity. Everyone wants to participate; everyone strikes a blow and, in order to do this, punches as near as he can to the victim. If he cannot hit himself, he wants to see others hit him. Every arm is thrust out as if they all belong to the same creature....*

— ELIAS CANETTI, CROWDS AND POWER

---

What's most pernicious about all this is that after it's over, there are no winners, despite the cheer of those declaring victory.

MOST SUCCESSFUL DEPLATFORMINGS ARE PYRRHIC VICTORIES

Here's why: let's step through the various participants in this and show how they undermined their own long term interests by doing this.

First, though, a quick word on Gab:

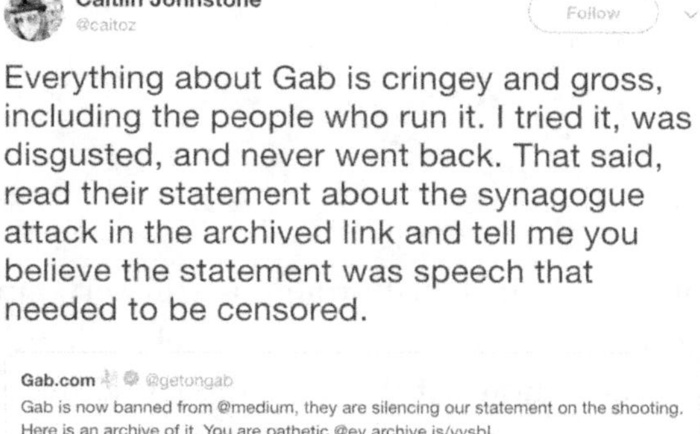


via http://twitter.com/caitoz/status/1056783477767471105

This mirrors my take on it when I created an account and took a look around. Gab illustrates a "catch-22" around setting out to be specifically a "free speech platform". You initially appeal to the most fringe elements of public discourse. Your first wave of users are going to be people for whom this has been a problem, and if you're an absolutist and let them on then suddenly that's your base. And once that's your base, it's a hard sell to entice the normies into the ecosystem. It's entirely understandable then, why Gab acquired a reputation for being an oasis of the alt-right. Adapting the "Pepe the Frog" meme as their logo didn't help. To many that looks like a dog whistle.

It all culminated, in the hours after the tragic shooting in Pittsburgh with their tweet about getting "1 million hits per hour" , possibly the stupidest thing ever tweeted, excepting maybe that time that guy tweeted a few jokes about the Ariana Grande concert bombing mere minutes after it happened...

All that said, their deplatforming is still very much troubling because they claim to have proactively aided the police once they became aware of the perpetrator's account on their system.

This is very much in line with how any other social media platform behaves, and is normal and responsible. Contrast Gab's cooperation in the Pittsburgh shooting investigation with the Daily Stormer who were widely deplatformed for going the extra mile to be indefensibly abominable pricks in the aftermath of Heather Heyer's murder in Charlottetown. Big difference, but same outcome.



**Stripe and PayPal:**

This one rattled me. We use Stripe. It's our main payment processor and probably the best we've ever worked with. But now they're making fairly loose judgment calls about their clients and letting the actions of a single downstream user, among thousands? (millions?) of a customer decide their fate? It sets a bad precedent. Same goes for PayPal.

Does this mean that if **Zerohedge,** or **Black Lives Matter,** two of our clients from opposite ends of the political spectrum, post something, or even if one of *their* users posts something, that is beyond the pale, then we have to worry about having our finances cut off?

I know as "the DNS guys" we have a near pathological aversion to single-points-of-failure, but it's not a stretch to come to the conclusion for any business that it's not an acceptable risk to have that possibility just looming there and to do nothing about it.

That means we will now be looking for backup payment processors. That means maybe after 20 years in business, maybe it's time to just pull it all in-house. Will any other businesses do the same? Anybody doing the same calculus will arrive at the same conclusion.

Stripe and PayPal put the question in their clients head every time they make a judgement call about one. Especially businesses built around downstream users.

**GoDaddy:**

Is known to skimp on due process[1] before unplugging any domains that garner any kind of quasi-official request , so it's no surprise that they cut loose Gab's domain. They're the 800-pound gorilla in the space and for them, I imagine that it's all a numbers game. It's just easier to kick them off than to *think* about whether they *should* kick them off.

Whenever I come across a fellow Libertarian, anarcho-capitalist, or even an Austrian-school economist or *any* kind of contrarian or heterodox voice, and I find out they're using GoDaddy, I caution them that they really are playing roulette. All it takes is some coordinated, well aimed outrage and they'll be gone.

And of course, there are groups out there whose entire raison d'être is to do just that.

**Shopify:**

Came under brief criticism for hosting Breitbart material, but they stuck it out, but this time they also deplatformed Gab.

Again – anybody using Shopify may want to rethink relying on them solely.

**Medium:**

Medium's suspensions I find quite troubling, considering that they banned Gab's official account where they would speak to the criticisms being levelled against themselves, but not rebroadcasting any of the material found on Gab that ostensibly made them problematic.

Caitlyn Johnstone was exactly correct when she drew attention specifically to Gab's statement on the Pittsburgh tragedy and posed the question: *what about that statement could possibly justify having their voice cut-off?*

As I write this, Twitter hasn't killed the Gab twitter account, yet. But they did seemingly coordinate with Facebook and others in the latest Facebook purge of FreeThoughtProject[2]. (I listened to an excellent interview with the co-founders on the Tom Woods podcast[3] this morning.)

Yes, all of the above are all within their rights to deplatform Gab. But all of the platforms that do so simply reinforce the notion in everybody's head: *these platforms have power over us,* and *they pose existential risk to our businesses or our ability to express ourselves.*

WHAT HAPPENS NEXT:

For that reason, countermeasures will emerge.

The traditional argument *"if you're doing nothing wrong, don't worry"* doesn't hold.

Maybe today, that means "if you are a social justice minded progressive you have nothing to worry about". But people forget that pendulums swing, history has certain cycles of mean reversion and then overshoot.

In the years after 9/11, I remember vividly how the neo-conservative narrative utterly dominated the mainstream media, and the word "liberal" was practically a slur. Those days are certainly gone. Do you think these days won't be?

What happens when everybody on the "safe" side of the narrative today is no longer considered acceptable tomorrow?

Personally, I think it's more pernicious than a mechanical back-and-forth struggle over control of the narrative. Left-vs-right is a false dichotomy. The real battle, the important one, is between those who would seek to decide what is acceptable for other people to think vs those who would rather think for themselves. It is centralization and consolidation vs decentralization and diversity.

The next challenger to Twitter will not be another centralized platform like Gab. It will be decentralized – perhaps a federation like Mastodon, where each node runs its own CoC and community standards – similar to IRC days. Or something blockchain based like Peepeth. Over all this recent attention around deplatforming, I've suddenly heard the name Mighty Networks more than once over the past few weeks. Turns out you can create your own network over there, and use your own domain to do it.

The tech giants today are by their own actions cultivating the motivation and the will to necessitate the creation of their own challengers and everybody is watching closely what works and what doesn't.

The next wave of disruption will not look like the last wave; the incumbent giants are not impervious to assault. I always like to remind people that Google, Facebook, Twitter, and the like may look unassailable today, but so did Yahoo and Myspace, yesterday.

The truly fringe discourse, the stuff nobody normal condones, will all go underground, where it will be harder to find and monitor and where it will revel in its inscrutability, metastasizing into God-knows-what from whence the occasional shock of really unhinged egregores will surely emerge.

APPENDIX B: SELECTED RESOURCES_

FREE SPEECH FRIENDLY WEB SERVICES

Here are some companies that are amenable to free speech and due process, spoiler alert, yes, I'm listing my own company in here.

List is in alphabetical order:

- easyDNS: Domains, DNS, Web hosting, Email (the author's company)
- Epik: domain registrar: free speech absolutist. They take on clients easyDNS won't.
- Gandi: domain registrar, web host. Inclusion here by reputation only, I don't know them.
- NearlyFreeSpeech: Nobody likes rules, but everybody has to have a few.
- Ortcloud.ch: Swiss-based high-end web hosting, very militant pro-customer, pro free speech.

## ALTERNATIVE NEWS & COMMENTARY

Here is a partial list of alternative media content producers I follow, read and recommend.

- #AxisOfEasy (by easyDNS, which is my company)
- Charles Hugh Smith
- David Stockman
- EpsilonTheory.com
- Foundation for Economic Education
- Guerrilla Capitalism (this is my blog)
- Hidden Forces
- The Intercept
- Metaviews
- Peak Prosperity
- Solari Report
- Tom Woods
- Zerohedge

# NOTES_

## INTRODUCTION

1. https://AxisOfEasy.com

## 1. FREEDOM IS A TWO-EDGED SWORD

1. John Whiteside Parsons, Freedom is a Two-Edged Sword
2. Ibid
3. Ibid
4. https://www.youtube.com/watch?v=52lcrzbfmhU
5. Janet Rietman, *Inside Scientology*. 2011 Rietman, 2013 Mariner Books

## 2. INVISIBLE MEN ARE NOT WELCOME IN THE PANOPTICON

1. China has started ranking citizens with a creepy 'social credit' system — here's what you can do wrong, and the embarrassing, demeaning ways they can punish you
   https://www.businessinsider.com/china-social-credit-system-punishments-and-rewards-explained-2018-4
2. https://www.chinalawtranslate.com/en/socialcreditsystem/
3. https://theintercept.com/2019/07/11/china-surveillance-google-ibm-semptian/
4. Omniphobic is a word, as far as I know, coined by myself to denote anything that somebody feels could be construed as hateful or intolerant. It doesn't matter what the "Omni" stands for. It can be anything and will eventually it include everything. "That which is not expressly permitted, will be forbidden".
5. https://tomwoods.com

## 3. CANCEL CULTURE THROUGH THE AGES

1. Haig Bosmajian, *Burning Books,* McFarland and Company, 2006.
2. Ibid
3. Ibid

4. Ibid

5. In the Sign of the Five, T. H. Meyer, 2014

6. https://www.nytimes.com/2019/12/23/world/middleeast/jamal-khashoggi-murder-sentence.html

7. https://www.theguardian.com/media/2019/nov/25/julian-assanges-health-is-so-bad-he-could-die-in-prison-say-60-doctors

8. Geek parlance for a "denial-of-service attack", originally meant to describe automated swarms of requests to overwhelm a target website or server

## 4. DOES DEPLATFORMING EVEN WORK?

1. https://www.techdirt.com/articles/20050105/0132239.shtml

2. Ibid

3. In the early 1990's, the then Premiere of Ontario, Bob Rae wrote a song about harmony and multiculturalism called "Same Boat Now". He submitted the song Sony Music and was rejected, prompting a small media circus along the theme of Mr. Rae not quitting his day job.

   The band I was in at the time, Landslide, from London, Ontario, recorded a punkish, power-pop version of the song, touching off a secondary, even larger media fracas. For awhile it looked like we would be able to parlay it into something, like a record deal... and then it all fizzled. Landslide was defunct a few months later.

   Somebody (not me) has since uploaded the song and the video we made for it to Youtube: http://urls.to/sameboatnow (we also didn't put the beginning text rant on that video).

4. Positive Effects of Negative Publicity: When Negative Reviews Increase Sales by Jonah Berger, Alan T. Sorensen & Scott J. Rasmussen. 2009.

   https://www.jonahberger.com/wp-content/uploads/2013/02/Negative_Publicity.pdf

5. https://thefreethoughtproject.com/

6. https://www.rollingstone.com/politics/politics-features/who-will-fix-facebook-759916/

7. https://www.dailymail.co.uk/news/article-6039753/Alex-Jones-says-5-6-million-people-subscribed-Infowars-Apple-ban.html

8. https://en.wikipedia.org/wiki/Paul_Bernardo

9. https://nowtoronto.com/news/paul-bernardo-s-mad-world-order/

10. it is important to understand, Julian Assange's subsequent flight and asylum within the Ecuadorian embassy were in response to sexual misconduct allegations in Sweden, of which there were never any charges entered. Assange sought asylum over fears the allegations were politically motivate and would result in his deportation to the US in

connection with the Wikileaks activities. Given that he is now in custody
facing this exact outcome, it appears he was not wrong.

11.  https://wikileaks.org/Banking-Blockade.html
12.  https://www.computerweekly.com/news/1280094508/Amazon-cloud-kicks-off-WikiLeaks-following-US-pressure
13.  https://www.theguardian.com/media/blog/2010/dec/03/wikileaks-knocked-off-net-dns-everydns
14.  https://www.bbc.com/news/business-22294108
15.  https://www.cnbc.com/2017/10/16/wikileaks-julian-assange-bitcoin-50000-percent-return-thanks-to-us-government.html
16.  https://www.ts.today/
17.  I have never been into gaming and the entire gamer culture is alien to me, so I have never even partially understood what "Gamergate" was all about. Different people involved in it will give you different versions of it. It is a highly polarizing topic amongst all involved. All I know is I don't know enough about it to comment intelligently.
18.  https://www.marketwatch.com/story/cloudflare-drops-8chan-as-a-client-after-mass-shootings-calling-it-a-cesspool-of-hate-2019-08-04
19.  https://8kun.net
20.  https://gab.ai
21.  https://easydns.com/blog/2018/11/02/a-heretics-guide-to-deplatforming/


## 5.  "OWN THE RACECOURSE"

1.  https://www.superfastbusiness.com/traffic/own-the-racecourse-training-introduction/


## 6.  ALWAYS PROMOTE YOUR OWN BRAND

1.  RSS is losing relevance as most browsers today have dropped support for it. But given how embedded it is across multiple systems, there will probably be RSS readers, and people who use them, for a long time. The larger point is to put options in front of people that they can use to keep connected to your material that isn't mediated by a centralized social media platform.


## 7.  WEBSITE HOSTING

1.  https://wordpress.org
2.  https://drupal.org

## 8. BLOGS

1. https://policies.google.com/terms?hl=en#toc-content

## 9. DISCUSSION FORUMS

1. http://allnewspipeline.com/Disqus_Attacking_Independent_Media.php
https://www.reddit.com/r/disqus/comments/
8fdoy1/disqus_censorship/
2. https://www.wpbeginner.com/opinion/switching-away-from-disqus-review-increased-comments-by-304/

## 10. YOUR EMAIL

1. https://AxisOfEasy.com
2. https://sendy.co/
3.
4. https://www.mautic.org/
5. https://easydns.com/blog/2019/07/15/paypal-phish-sent-to-easydns-zoneedit-customers/
6. https://geekflare.com/self-hosted-marketing-email/
7. Managing Mission Critical Domains & DNS, Jeftovic, 2018. Packt Publishing
8. https://www.quora.com/Are-the-Wikileaks-Podesta-emails-genuine
9. https://mailgun.com
10. https://sendgrid.com
11. https://postageapp.com/
12. https://easydns.com/email/easyoutbound-smtp-service/

## 11. PODCASTING

1. https://www.cnet.com/news/apple-has-dropped-alex-jones-and-infowars-from-itunes-podcasts/
2. https://solari.com
3. https://www.forumborealis.net/
4. https://contrakrugman.com
5. https://www.stitcher.com/

## 12. ECOMMERCE SOLUTIONS

1. A Heretic's Guide to Deplatforming
   https://easydns.com/blog/2018/11/02/a-heretics-guide-to-deplatforming/
2. https://guerrilla-capitalism.com/articles/get-thee-a-backup-payment-gateway/
3. Get Thee a Backup Payment Gateway
   https://guerrilla-capitalism.com/articles/get-thee-a-backup-payment-gateway/


## 13. BAD REVENUE MODELS

1. Dilbert cartoonist Scott Adams has done a few periscopes on this (I don't know if Twitter's Periscope can be monetized. If it can, then it belongs on this list as well).
2. https://dailycaller.com/2018/07/16/sleeping-giants-founder-rivitz/
3. https://www.youtube.com/watch?v=YmcK6GvgVPs
4. https://www.youtube.com/watch?v=YmcK6GvgVPs
5. Ibid
6. https://www.breitbart.com/tech/2019/06/13/exclusive-facebooks-process-to-label-you-a-hate-agent-revealed/
7. https://www.theverge.com/2017/11/16/16667668/twitter-verification-removal-judge-offline-behavior
8. https://www.subscribestar.com/?sref=8DXV
9. https://www.subscribestar.com/guidelines
10. https://bitbacker.io
11. https://itsgoingdown.org
12. https://deflect.ca
13. https://www.washingtontimes.com/news/2019/jun/29/andy-ngo-beaten-up-by-antifa-activists-at-portland/
14. https://www.rollingstone.com/culture/culture-features/andy-ngo-right-wing-troll-antifa-877914/


## 14. GOOD REVENUE MODELS

1. https://letstalkbitcoin.com
2. https://tomwoods.com
3. https://pathstoincome.com/

## 15. SECURING YOUR DOMAIN NAMES

1. No, it wasn't QuadrigaCX, although we worked with them too, doing takedowns on phishing sites before it all went bust.
2. https://easydns.com/blog/2018/07/18/new-book-managing-mission-critical-domains-dns/
3. http://readthis.ca/dnsbook
4. A Canary email is when you use a unique email address for every different vendor. You can use a dedicated domain, such as "marks-email.com" and then use addresses like gmail@marks-email.com, facebook@marks-email.com, etc. You can also use what's called "unix plus notation", i.e. given my email markjr@easydns.com, I could use markjr+facebook@easydns.com, markjr+itunes@easydns.com, etc). The latter *should* work everwhere, but you occasionally come across web forms and even the odd mail server that doesn't.
5. https://www.icann.org/resources/pages/tdrp-2016-06-01-en
6. https://easydns.com/wp-content/uploads/2019/05/easyDNS_Technologies_Decision_FA_1532690.pdf
7. https://www.icann.org/resources/pages/tdrp-2016-06-01-en
8. https://www.icann.org/resources/pages/providers-fc-2012-02-25-en
9.
10. http://techland.time.com/2011/02/23/if-libya-falls-what-happens-to-all-those-twitter-bit-ly-links/
11. https://thenextweb.com/socialmedia/2010/10/08/libyas-clarifies-the-vb-ly-takedown-bit-ly-can-breathe-easy/
12. https://www.theregister.co.uk/2019/05/27/io_domains_uk_un/

## 16. BACKING IT ALL UP

1. Torn: A Forensic Romance. VP Media https://applewhite.ca

## 17. ALTERNATIVE PLATFORMS

1. https://telegram.org
2. https://www.zerohedge.com/political/zerohedge-suspended-twitter
3. https://t.me/zh_chat
4. https://keybase.io
5. https://www.minds.com/content-policy
6. https://peepeth.com
7. https://peepeth.com/help/mobile
8. https://metamask.io

### FIRST THEY CAME FOR THE FILE SHARING DOMAINS

1. https://encyclopedia.ushmm.org/content/en/article/martin-niemoeller-first-they-came-for-the-socialists

### THE CULTURAL PURGE WILL NOT BE TELEVISED

1. https://news.ycombinator.com/item?id=13744694

### A HERETIC'S GUIDE TO DEPLATFORMING

1. https://easydns.com/blog/2014/08/02/is-your-domain-name-safe-from-nefarious-interests/
2. https://thefreethoughtproject.com/
3. excellent interview with the co-founders on the Tom Woods podcast